To Ch ✍ **W9-CUJ-936**

Bury My Heart in Boulder

Best Wishes
Lord Bless you
Mitch

Bury My Heart in Boulder

Memoirs of a Big-8 Conference Football Walk-on Linebacker

by Marty Cone

Xulon Press

Xulon Press
2301 Lucien Way #415
Maitland, FL 32751
407.339.4217
www.xulonpress.com

© 2017 by Marty Cone

All rights reserved solely by the author. The author guarantees all
contents are original and do not infringe upon the legal rights of
any other person or work. No part of this book may be reproduced
in any form without the permission of the author. The views
expressed in this book are not necessarily those of the publisher.

Scripture quotations taken from the Holy Bible, New International
Version (NIV). Copyright © 1973, 1978, 1984, 2011 by Biblica,
Inc.™. Used by permission. All rights reserved.

Printed in the United States of America.

ISBN-13: 9781545611807

To everyone out there who inspired me in all

my athletic endeavors

and to my wife and children.

Contents

Preface

I was the youngest senior to graduate from my high school class. For the first half of 12th grade, I was 16 years old. Everybody told me "nice job on your athletic career, but now you're done." I wasn't done with sports, but everyone else insisted I was.

Do you have a voice inside you that says, "I'm not finished yet"? Do you feel you can go on to the next level even though the odds are stacked against you? Are you willing to sacrifice in order to follow your dreams?

This book is for you. Trust me, you will regret it for the rest of your life if you don't at least try. Don't let anyone convince you otherwise. Hard work is its own reward, and sacrifice and commitment can change your life. They have enabled me to accomplish what most people thought was impossible. This book isn't only for the high school and college athlete but for anyone who has a goal in life. You've put that goal off long enough. Start tomorrow! Scratch that – start today!

Let this be your year. Silence the critics. Go for it. With God's help, you can do all things. I was and am very blessed. I hope you enjoy the encouragement and the laughter. More than that, I hope my story inspires you.

Marty Cone

Forward

I have a few questions for you. Were you a starter your junior year of high school only to get hurt and sit out most of your senior year? Were you the second or third fastest in your region, barely missing qualifying for the state competition? Were you disqualified for pulling a muscle at an important meet? Were you overlooked after your high school team underwent a coaching change? Did your coach tell you that you had a bad attitude? Was the player in front of you ever chosen over you even though you knew you were better – possibly because the coach had grown up with that other player's parents? Did you ever lose by one point or one stroke? Did you ever have to sit out due to a bad grade? Did you ever miss a complete season because you had to work to help support your family?

Have you ever watched someone take state as a senior who you had beat as a junior? Have you ever injured yourself having fun during the off-season? Did your letters and videos go unanswered by the colleges to which they were sent? Have you ever had a collegiate coach write or call to let you know that you were a victim of a numbers game and that no openings were available? Have you ever re-emerged two years later, 30 pounds heavier, three seconds faster, and 40 pounds stronger?

Have you ever felt that you haven't reached your potential and that your best years are still in front of you?

I want to encourage you to believe in yourself. Hopefully my story can help. I wish you faith, perseverance, and the best of luck.

CHAPTER 1

Courtside at the ABA Game

Junior high is a trying time for any young man. There are girls to impress, new blemishes breaking out, and bullies around every hallway. Many of us ninth graders spent our days working through these issues.

I was asked to the ninth grade dance by this girl named Sue. I was a bit leery as she had already lettered in making out. We made plans to meet at the dance on Friday at four, but on the way I decided to play basketball with my friends instead. The following Monday she was still pretty fired up about it and shoved me into a locker in front of my friends. How I wanted to give her a few chops. Kung fu and Bruce Lee were the hottest tickets in town, and after watching many of these movies my gang and I were feeling pretty tough. And I was finally up to 100 pounds of body weight. But I maintained my composure.

One day, my neighbor and best friend, Jim Capra, told me he had three tickets to the Denver Rockets basketball game. His mom was working at the game and could seat us down by the court. We called our dear friend Eric Chester and invited him too. Once I got permission from my folks, Eric's sister dropped us off at the Denver Auditorium Arena. Cadillacs and limos lined the streets, along with big afros and long leather jackets. Music played as we were seated just two rows from the brand-new wooden court. The arena was a spectacle for all to see. The uniforms were dazzling. The ball was red, white, and blue, and three pointers were allowed along with six fouls. The level of excitement was much higher than the modern-day NBA. The ABA was truly the golden era of basketball.

The national anthem played, fans were seated, and the ball was tipped. Denver's point guard was a splendid athlete named Ralph Simpson. He had gone to Detroit City's Pershing High School. His teammate Spencer Haywood was another super-star. Together they had won the coveted Michigan High School Basketball Championship. After two strong years at Michigan State, Ralph had signed with the Denver Rockets. Attendance was now at an all-time high.

I sat on the edge of my seat as Ralph dribbled the ball past us several times. I had to restrain myself from actually reaching out and touching him.

His defender was a Virginia Squire, another talented athlete. The defender covered him a bit too close. Before the first quarter was over, Ralph and his defender suddenly started slapping each other and fell to the floor in a knockdown drag-out fight. I couldn't just sit there – I had to help my point guard.

I leaped over the row in front of me onto the court and joined the fray. I swung wildly and tried to hold my own, but I was sandwiched between the two players on the floor. Before I knew it, I was being dragged out of the mix by a ref who had me by the foot. I staggered back to my seat as the players were separated. Eric and Jim couldn't believe what I had done. I couldn't believe it either. I sat there in fear, knowing the police would be coming for me.

Things cooled off, and I figured I was safe. Then at halftime three guys tapped me on the shoulder and asked me to come with them. I figured I was either being sent home or to jail. But when we got to the top of the stairs, one of them handed me a hot dog and Pepsi and said, "Thank you. I saw what you did, and we all appreciate it." What a relief.

Anytime I was around Eric we were constantly trying to outdo each other. That day I had outdone him. If our dads had ever found out, it would have been curtains for all of us.

CHAPTER 2

It Was On

···•··

When I finished junior high, I received an award as the only four-sport athlete. At 5'6" inches, weighing in at 105 pounds, I wasn't an imposing figure. Finally at age 13 my voice was starting to change. The next three years would be the defining years of my life.

Jim Capra invited Eric Chester and me to another ABA game. We gladly said yes. Jim's mom worked the doors and got us in for free just like last year. Eric's mom dropped us off, and now we were on our own. I promised them both that I would stay clear of any fights. The game was held at the Denver Auditorium Arena again. The division-leading Kentucky Colonels were in town. It had been a year since my last scuffle there, and I was a lot more mature now, practically grown up.

It was a great game with several lead changes. Denver prevailed in the end. Afterward, Jim and I positioned ourselves in front of the portal to give high fives to the Kentucky Colonels as they walked off the court. I figured all those players would want to give me a high five. I still had some things to learn about life.

The first player to come off was Dan Issel. He honored me with a high five. Next was 7'2" inch Artis Gilmore and then Louie Dampier, both with high fives. Rick Mount, Kentucky's talented point guard, gave me a dirty look and walked right past, leaving me hanging with my hand in the air. So I shoved him as his instep was in the air, and he fell over.

Suddenly it was on. Rick chased me across the court, over the bleachers, back down across the court, under the basket, back across the court, past the cheerleaders, past the police, and under the bleachers! I could hear people screaming. He finally stopped his pursuit as he wasn't willing to dive under the bleachers to get me. If he would have caught me, I would have been dead. The papers would have read, "Thirteen-year-old boy beaten nearly half to death by enraged ABA player."

To this day, I don't know what compelled me to do such a thing. I have always wanted to apologize for my actions, as Rick was a fierce competitor. So Rick, if you're out there, I'm sorry. I had never been seen as a troublemaker or bad kid. I just needed to learn to channel my emotions.

CHAPTER 3

Getting Bolder in Boulder

I was 14 years old and a sophomore in high school. I had calmed down some, and I was making better decisions and starting to mature. Our high school varsity basketball team was playing in Boulder, Colorado, that very Friday night. All my friends were either too busy or couldn't make the game, but oh how I wanted to go. Boulder was only 30 minutes away from Wheat Ridge, where I lived. It was practically in my own backyard.

It was approaching six, and to my surprise my parents told me to keep an eye on my younger siblings, as they were on their way to my dad's annual office party. The wheels started to turn. I struck a bargain – for two chocolate candy bars, my little sister and brother would let me leave for two hours. I grabbed the car keys, and off to Boulder I drove. With two or three hours of practice driving the vehicle up and down the driveway, I felt I had a reasonable amount of experience. Still, I was a little nervous at 14 driving up the Boulder Turnpike at 70 miles per hour. I sat on the yellow pages to gain a little height. My confidence in the Oldsmobile Delta 88 was high. Under the hood sat a 455 Rocket engine.

Before I knew it, I found the Boulder High parking lot and carefully parked what I considered my parents' "big rig." The game was well into the first quarter by the time I found several of my friends. People were flipping out as I showed up with car keys in my hand. I could only stay till halftime as my nerves were getting a little tight, and I felt like throwing up.

I left just 30 minutes after I had arrived. A friend had told me to head straight east as it would be safer to stay away from the turnpike. After heading straight east for about 20 minutes, I was getting a bit nervous. My landmark of Wadsworth Boulevard was nowhere in sight. I was now lost in the pitch black of night and getting really scared. I saw a farmhouse just off the road to my right. There looked to be a party going on, so I pulled into the drive to ask directions. Ice was everywhere, and once I parked the car was stuck.

I ran down the driveway to the side door where I saw several cars and heard loud music playing. I knocked frantically, but nobody answered. I was in tears and knew I had gotten myself into a big jam. As I walked back to the car, a spirit

7

of calm suddenly came over me. My older brother, Tom, had taught me that if I ever got stuck I should simply rock the car back and forth from drive to reverse. Less than a minute later I was free.

I backed up safely onto the road, almost forgetting to thank those fine people for helping me in my darkest hour. Leaving the Delta 88 up on the road in park, I ran down to the house and threw a gigantic rock through the front glass door of the house where the party was raging. I then sprinted back to the car and drove the Delta 88 east at 88 miles an hour. Before I knew it, I was almost home with only one more hurdle to cross. Coming up over a hill less than four blocks from my house, I slid off the road. I smashed my dad's front blinker light. More than that, I plowed into the side of a hippie-looking parked van. I hope the people had insurance because I didn't. Thank God I made it home safely. Inside, I sat shaking for the next half hour, constantly looking outside to make sure I was safe.

Next time, I'll gladly take a ride, I thought.

I never really got to see Boulder in the dark, but I heard it was nice.

CHAPTER 4

Are You Ready for Some Football?

The Denver Broncos would be taking on the Oakland Raiders. We couldn't wait for the game. Monday Night Football was a big hit and had the best sportscasters in America, including Frank Gifford, Don Meredith, and Howard Cosell.

These were the turbulent 70s, and we all needed a little extra money and a laugh, so I began to wonder how much could I could make if I ran across the field on Monday night during the game. I asked my friend Jim Capra if he was in, and he was, so I asked around to see how much people would give us to run across the field. The response was overwhelming. More than 200 people offered me 25 cents, 50 cents, 75 cents, one dollar, McDonald's lunches, movie tickets. Most friends thought we would never make it across or that we would just flat chicken out. It was on. I knew I could do it – I just hoped my parents wouldn't be able to recognize one of their seven children on national television. Jim was afraid his dad would find out. His dad, Leonard Capra, was a high school teacher and had been a fierce competitor all of his years.

The first hurdle was to get into the stadium with no tickets and no money. Jim and I stood alongside one of the 80-foot-tall steel beams holding up Mile High Stadium. The crowd filing into Mile High was going absolutely wild, people screaming, whistles blowing, and bands playing. What a perfect night for a game.

As kickoff approached, Jim and I had to move quickly. We scaled the beam like two squirrels. Once we made it onto the second level, we dispersed into the crowd. By the time the cops saw us, we were way up on the third level. I couldn't resist grabbing a couple of coffee creamers from the concession stand on the third floor and flinging them over the wall down on the crowd. By now, a great game was just underway. John Madden was coaching up a storm, and the Broncos were holding their own.

Jim and I stood behind the Raiders' bench. Our cue was the start of the fourth quarter, when all eyes would be on us. As the third quarter ended, I leaped over the fence and stood next to Kenny Stabler, Oakland's famous quarterback. I was now the newest member of the Oakland Raiders. I looked back at my pal Jim, who had chickened out.

I had a backup plan just in case. I jumped back into the crowd, hoping no one would grab us and haul us away. I grabbed Jim's wallet and threw it onto the 40 yard line. Jim realized that he had to come with me, so up and over the fence we went. Jim grabbed his wallet, and off we ran all the way across the field.

The police were real nice. It only took six of Denver's finest to subdue us and remove us from the field. We could hear the announcer and the late Bob Martin on the radio encouraging the cops to take us to jail. Howard Cosell called us "two young inconsiderates." He was wrong; I was very considerate to make sure Jim made it across. You see, Howard Cosell didn't need the extra dough like we did.

As we were being escorted down the sideline, I looked clear up to the corner of the upper level to see the funniest thing ever. It was the Dampier family giving us a standing ovation. Thank goodness the police only threw us out of the stadium and didn't haul us to jail. Once we were outside, we quickly snuck back in.

I could hardly sleep that night knowing of the windfall I would receive the next day. As Jim and I entered our high school, the lobby was full of our classmates. The money came pouring in, and I collected my bounty. I had free lunches for a month, movie tickets, and lots of cash. My dad suspected I was up to no good but never confronted me. Maybe he realized that I had been doing a lot of growing up.

CHAPTER 5

A Run-in with Chuck Mandrill

I attended Jefferson High School (10th, 11th, and 12th grade) in a Denver suburb called Edgewater. I loved my high school, especially all of us growing up together like a close-knit family. I lived in east Wheat Ridge, home of Wheat Ridge High School, which was our rival known for such athletes as Lee Kunz (who later played for the Chicago Bears), Dave Logan (Cleveland Browns), Terry Kunz (Oakland Raiders), and Bill Leary (Denver Broncos). Wheat Ridge was loaded with as much talent as any school in the country. These boys were truly great athletes, around 6'4" and well over 200 pounds.

They were also real good looking and not welcome at our school. All our girls would go absolutely crazy when they would come to Jefferson High to compete against us.

As Jim and I were walking home one day, we threw snowballs at cars. Suddenly, a huge, muscled monster got out of one of the cars and chased us down. He outran us and grabbed us both. We were pretty scared. He walked us back to his car and threw us into the backseat. I remember him asking, "Who do you think you are, pelting my car with snowballs?" Looking toward the back window I noticed a CU football helmet.

"Who are you, and what are going to do to us?" I asked.

He said, "I'm taking you to your house."

We knew our parents would have killed us, so we gave him a phony address. I ended up directing him to three different houses, telling him I wasn't really sure where I lived. After awhile, he got angry about driving in circles. He finally parked in front of some old lady's house, which I thought was funny. We apologized to him, and he let us go. He warned us to never hit his car again and told us both to grow up.

Later we found out his name was Chuck Mandrill, captain of the University of Colorado football team. He was an offensive guard, 6'3" and 265 pounds of solid rock muscle and a fellow Jefferson High alum. Later on we would become great friends. Several surgeries ultimately cut his pro football career short. He also had a sister in my high school class who was extremely hot but wouldn't respond to my pleas.

Sophomore football was a blast. I played guard and defensive lineman. Our coach, Mike Carter, took Jim and me aside and told us we were the two toughest kids he had ever coached. I felt pretty tough even though I could only bench press my body weight – 115 pounds. Still, Coach Carter was young, and I figured he hadn't coached long enough to make such a statement.

Coach Carter would nonetheless have a lasting impact on my life, as he would teach us about work ethic, weightlifting, and the importance of being quality citizens.

CHAPTER 6

Veggie and Big Larry

M y buddy Ron and I standing around in Veggie's class my junior year talking about baseball. Our teacher was nicknamed "Veggie" because he refused to eat beef of any sort. Veggie was from New York City and kept himself in great shape. He was a great teacher and a scrappy, feisty sort of dude. Veggie was also the girls' head basketball coach. He always managed to get his team to the playoffs.

As the bell rang, we all were seated. Five minutes into the class period, in walked 6'5" Big Larry, who had a mind of his own. It was the sixth or seventh day Larry had showed up late, as he was always just outside the door mugging on his girl- friend. Every day they'd be swallowing each other's faces in the middle of the hall for all the free world to see, which was pretty gross. (I also always thought she could have prettied herself up a little more, as her hair was always a mess.) Every day Big Larry arrived late, I felt that an apology was in order, but Larry never gave Veggie so much as an "excuse me." Ron and I knew there would be trouble ahead.

Next thing you know, Larry and Veggie were face to face in front of the class. Words were exchanged, and the two started throwing punches and wrestling all over the ground. Larry looked like a jigsaw puzzle with a couple of pieces gone, which shocked everyone because Veggie was only 5'9". Ron and I had to act quick to separate the two. Next thing we knew, we were walking them both to the principal's office. It was a hard decision to make because we loved both guys.

In the days that followed, Ron and I often thought that we should have just let them cool off instead of taking them to the principal. After a day or two, class resumed, and everything was back to normal. Larry was the first one to get to class from then on, leaving his poor gal begging for more out in the hallway.

Chapter 7

Marty's Done

By my junior year, I was working out as hard as I could. I would do 100 pushups three nights per week. Summer evenings, I would sneak out of my house two times per week at 11 p.m. to run five miles around Sloan's Lake, sometimes with ankle weights on. I would arrive back at home around midnight, and my parents would never know I had been gone, mainly because my brother Tom and I always slept out on our front porch. As a junior I was starting varsity linebacker at the age of 15. I led our team in tackles. I was also a starting varsity wrestler and starting left fielder in baseball. I felt even bigger as a starter, lining up behind my older brother Tom and all my buddies who controlled the defensive line. Tom was 6'1" and weighed around 235 pounds, and he was one of the toughest dudes in all of Jefferson County. I was only 5'7" and 130 pounds, but my bench press swelled to 170 pounds.

I started to get a little more respect from my upper class-mates. Feeling perhaps overconfident, I asked a fine-looking senior-class girl with beautiful red hair to homecoming. I knew full well she would love to go with me, only to be crushed when she said "no." No reason was cited, but I found out she liked some skanky-looking dude from another high school.

By my senior year, I was working out even harder. My bench press was now just over 200 pounds. I had never before worked as hard as I did that summer, drinking protein powder and never missing a workout. My strength coach, Paul Johnson, would always encourage me and have an extra box of protein to sell to me for $4, along with desiccated liver tablets, which were real big back then. With the protein and liver, I shot up to 5'8" and 142 pounds for the start of my senior-year campaign.

The football program had me listed at 5'10", 150 pounds. My bench press was up to 250 pounds. My parallel squat was 350 pounds, and my dead lift was 405 pounds. I was able to do 100 parallel dips in my backyard. I threw the softball 90 yards, leading all the gym classes. I was now doing 250 pushups three nights per week. I could do 1,000 pushups in one hour.

I had a great senior year at linebacker, and my teammates voted me captain. I had at least two interceptions each year. The previous year I had led the team with 60 tackles, and my senior year I was fortunate enough to lead the state with 118 tackles and 69 assists. I had more than 20 tackles in three different games. I had close to 10 tackles for a loss, which helped me achieve second team all-conference. The player who beat me out for all-state was 6'2" and around 220 pounds. Many college questionnaires came my way, but I think the colleges were put off by my size.

Baseball was perhaps my first love. I remember batting around 700 for the first half of the season. Towards the end of my senior year, I placed second in the state at the Colorado High School powerlifting championships. My bench press was about 275 pounds. Parallel squat was around 400, and dead lift was 500 pounds.

My brother Tom was 13 months older, weighing in at 235 pounds. I knew I would grow like he had. For now I would have to be patient. I charted my size, strength, and competitive spirit so I could compare my stats over the years.

As college rejection letters trickled in, I became discouraged and had to come up with a plan. My Uncle Harlas wanted me to play for him at William Jewell College in Liberty, Missouri. More than a few people told me my playing days were over. I'll never forget going to the high school weight room after I graduated that summer. My strength coach, Paul Johnson, said, "Wow, look how you have improved." And then the head football coach said, "Marty's done."

Talk about motivation – little did the head coach know it, but he had just inspired me to take on a huge series of challenges for the next eight years of my life.

The very next day, I met with Paul. I shook his hand and told him I was off to the United States Air Force and that my goal was to walk on at the University of Colorado when I got out.

He said, "Wow, if anyone can do it, Cone, it's you!"

Off I went with four boxes of protein, which he sold me from his desk drawer for $16. He threw in a box of desiccated liver tablets for free. I figured if the liver pills could make test rats swim longer, maybe they could have a positive effect on me.

Ever since I had been tossed in the backseat of Chuck Mandrill's car and seen that CU helmet, I knew where I wanted to go. I wasn't finished; I was on a mission. I was tired of everyone's opinion, and I had all the self-motivation I needed. I didn't even bother telling anyone else about my long-range plan because most would have thought I was dreaming. I also learned along the way that most people really don't care if you succeed or not.

On the way home later that afternoon, I thought I would pay the Lopez brothers a visit. Louie was my age and Mark was 2 years younger. Our relatives were from the same area near Trinidad Colorado. I had borrowed my mom's 1969 Mercury Cougar and was ready to take them for a spin. Mr. Lopez greeted me at the door and told me the boys were downstairs.

Their basement was small and I had to watch my step. But I found them lounging in the TV room. I was all excited to get going but neither of their lazy butts wanted to go. I had to beg them 4 times before they finally gave in.

Reluctantly they followed me to the car. As they entered I showed them a "surprise" I had for them. A beautiful creature looking mask and a long trench coat. We drove only a couple of miles and were now in front of the beautiful, brand new, Casa Bonita Restaurant. It had been recently built and there was crowd 2 blocks long. Inside the Restaurant were gunfighters, cliff divers, and roving Mariachi bands. It was an enormous attraction. I had another one of my great ideas to make the Lopez brothers laugh. Just next to the long line of customers were a group of 5 payphones I got out of the car and walked into the nearest payphone. After a short struggle, I emerged with my Monster Mask on and my Trench Coat nicely buttoned. Finally I had the Lopez brothers laughing as I walked up and down the sidewalk making kids and customers laugh.

The fun lasted only about 3-4 minutes when suddenly out of nowhere, we were surrounded by the Lakewood Police Department. Over a dozen police cars rolled up. Over the loud speaker I heard, "All of you, on the ground with your hands in the air." Just what the Lopez brothers needed on that peaceful afternoon. Now we all 3 were thrown into the back of the police car. The Lopez brothers were in handcuffs but I never got cuffed. The Officer in the driver's seat was asking way too many questions as he filled out his report. He was getting mad at the Lopez Boys because they were so mad that they did not want to answer. Deep inside I knew we could not get in trouble as we were only having fun. I told the officer that I had a personal question for him. He said, "What is it?" I then asked him, "Has anybody ever told you that you look like Barney Fife." Boy that really helped as he threatened me, and told me to shut my mouth. I had the boys laughing out loud, and uncontrollably. After a few more questions I then asked him, "Do they allow you only 1 bullet in your gun or is it your pocket?" That helped even more. He was now furious and warned me that one more word would put me in the crossbar hotel overnight. My mind said, "Whatever." Mark was in the middle seat with his muscular tricep cuffed behind his back and yet within biting distance, I was getting bored with the line of questioning so here it comes. I reached over and bit Mark in the left tricep pretty hard. So hard that He screamed in the officer's ear. The cop threw down the clipboard, reached back and got Mark in a headlock. Then I got involved separating the cop from Mark. Another Officer saw the scuffle and came running over, took us all out, and demanded to know what was going on. Mark told the cop that I bit him in the arm and I said, "Prove it." Mark showed the officer his arm, the bite mark were easy to see. I told the cop, "He bit me first." All the officers met for a few more minutes and then decided to release us. All the way home the Lopez boys did not say one word to me. Then when they home we all fell onto the ground and we laughed for 15 minutes. The Police Department took my mask and my trench coat and warned me, "never again."

I would miss high school, some of the most fun years of my life. I know most of the staff would be glad to see my gang and me leave, as we had plotted and carried out at least a prank a day. We had had a blast! Now I was ready for whatever would come next.

CHAPTER 8

U.S. Air Force Boot Camp

Off to Lackland Air Force Base, in San Antonio, Texas. I was 17. Both of my parents had to co-sign for my enlistment. My father, Ray, is a retired Air Force E-9 Chief Master Sergeant, and he encouraged me to join. The military was good to him, and he proudly served for 21 years. He's from Jacksonville, Texas, and he entered the military at 15 years of age, telling the recruiter that he had just turned 18.

It was my first time leaving home, yet after I got over the initial shock I believed I would have the time of my life. There's nothing in my life I've been more proud of than serving my country. Few days have gone by when I haven't thought about the military, especially when I see a nation at war. I gained the highest possible respect for our troops, our training, our flag, and our president. I want to thank each and every soldier, enlisted person, officer, and National Guard member for their sacrifice and service to our country. To all the veterans and to the families of those who served and who died, I love you all. God bless you and our beautiful nation. Every day I pray for the wounded and disabled.

There I was on my first day of boot camp in the U.S. Air Force. All 70 of my fellow recruits were telling stories of just how great they were before their enlistment. Now we were off to the barbershop for our first haircut. If you had any warts, moles, or growths on your head, you had to point to them or else they would be shaved off in seconds. Then we were off to the uniform factory for our combat fatigue uniforms. All these tough guys were now reduced to no more than a bunch of bald men in green suits. No more biker jackets, running shoes, or tank tops – we were all the same now.

Boot camp was tough on me. I'll never forget on the fourth day of boot camp while I was standing outside in line waiting to march into the dining hall. A group of six or seven soldiers approached and asked if anybody was hoping to be military police. Naturally, I jumped out of line and said I was. They told me that if I really wanted to make an impression on my drill instructor, then I should tuck my pants inside of my boots. I felt that was pretty good advice as they had their pants neatly tucked inside their boots, so off to the dining hall I marched with my pants tucked in my boots. I piled on a huge amount of food and headed to my seat. I walked by the drill instructors' table, several of whom were now looking only at me. In a flash, I was ordered to put my food down and stand in front of their table at full attention. Twelve different drill instructors took turns ripping into me with insults and verbal abuse in front of 500 soldiers. I felt about two inches tall.

They must have had a pretty good time showing off in front of each other. How I wanted to say something, but already I knew better. I quickly learned that "discretion is the better part of valor." They were all super tough, and many were former Marines. I learned never to listen to passersby. In the meantime, I took my pants out of my boots.

About four weeks into boot camp, our commander told us one morning that we needed to get in the best physical shape we could for the upcoming U.S. Air Force physical records challenge. The mile record was 4:35, the sit-up record was 1,000, and the pushup record was 167. In my mind, all three records were all up for grabs.

That week, we got our first town pass. Eight of us airmen decided to stay in and write letters to our families and continue training for the upcoming challenge, which we figured was two or three weeks away. I did 100 pushups without stopping, my former record being 110. I continued on and got to 150. Suddenly all of my friends started to cheer me on. I kept going, reaching 160, 170, 180, 200, 210, and finally 220, at which point I collapsed. My chest and triceps were in severe pain. I felt like I had ripped open my entire upper body. As the rest of the airmen returned from town, they heard the news and were excited for me, as I had unofficially broken the Air Force record, which had stood for more than 30 years. I was shocked that I had doubled my personal record. As I went to bed that night, I had no idea what would lie in store for me the next day.

The following morning at 0500 hours, with our usual rude awakening, an announcement came over the loudspeaker: "Anyone who thinks they can break any of the U.S. Air Force fitness records head downstairs." No one had known that the tests would take place the very next morning. My entire flight of 70 soldiers came by and shook my hand. They knew I was still recovering from my new unofficial record the night before. Competition would be fierce, as two to three thousand airmen would be giving it their best shot.

At 11:15 a.m., we got the news over the intercom that the mile record had fallen with a time of four minutes 17 seconds by a fellow named Stancyk from back east. He had done it wearing combat boots. At 2 p.m., we got the news over the loudspeaker that the sit-up record had fallen, the new record being 2,000. The record holder claimed his dad would make his entire family do 1,000 sit-ups every night before they went to bed.

The heat was on. They kept calling out, "Can't anyone do more than 90 push- ups? Are you afraid? Are there any real men on this base?" At 4 p.m., some guys in my flight encouraged me to at least give it a try.

Now, triceps don't heal overnight; you need to give them a couple days' rest. I went to the corner of the barracks and somehow did 40. I felt no pain whatsoever. At 17, this might have been my first test of mind over matter.

As I walked down into the charge of quarters, I noticed a portrait on the wall. It was General John Flynn, our base commander. My dad had told me about him when I was younger. General Flynn had been shot down over North Vietnam in an F-105 Thunderchief fighter jet. He had been a prisoner of war for five years. I thought about his sacrifice and his beautiful family who had desperately awaited his return. I was now so psyched up that I could hardly wait. I knew I was going to smash the record. My adrenalin kicked in before I even started. It was a strange feeling.

A group of fitness officers directed me in. My phys. ed. sergeant gave me his usual derogatory greeting. He told me that the Air Force pushup record of 167 hadn't been broken in 30 years and said I was wasting his time. He went on and on about what a puss I looked like. I reassured him that he could continue his comments later on, but for now I meant business. I had never felt this way before, and I couldn't reel myself back in. He made me remove my belt buckle so I wouldn't scratch the polished floor. It was on!

With 15 people and cameras looking on, all I had to do was supply the body and triceps. I was so fired up with all their insults that I hit 50 with the greatest of ease. Then 100. And then I couldn't feel a thing. Then 120, then 130, and then the instructors began to scream. Several officers were on the floor, practically on top of me, screaming, "GO! GO! GO!" I hit 140, 150, 160, 180, 200, mass hysteria all around me. Everyone was going crazy! They were screaming in my ears, 220, 230, 240. Finally I collapsed at 249.

They were all so proud because I represented their squadron, 3708 BMTS. I couldn't believe I could do that many pushups after the unofficial record I had set the night before. All the commanders told me to relax and stay right where I was. Within minutes, newspaper reporters and cameramen were all over the place. I later found out that this was the record everybody had wanted to see broken for the last several years. My fitness instructor believed it wasn't only an Air Force record but a new world record as well. It was all confusion to me, as I was just grateful to be able to complete the pushups at all!

Back at barracks, all my fellow airmen were going nuts. They were in shock that I had been able to compete. My celebrity status was on the rise, and I no longer had to march, give blood, or clean the latrines. I was able to eat at different dining halls and be treated like a king. Two weeks later I would receive my orders for my security police school assignment just 40 miles away. I had passed the test for the elite pararescue unit but was turned down due to asthma problems, which they later found out were nothing more than allergies.

After boot camp, I was sent to Camp Bullis, Texas, for Air Base Ground Defense school, night maneuvers, and weapons training. During six weeks of sleeping in a freezing cold tent, I was still able to do pushups and chin-ups near the showers late at night. Several young men joined me to get nice and buff before they went home for Christmas. Being close to sea level, I was able to run a 5:15 mile in combat boots. I felt myself separating from the rest of the pack as I saw little motivation in many of the other soldiers. Competition was in my blood.

The next day, I threw a live grenade 80 yards, setting the camp record. After six months, I was ordered to my permanent assignment at a huge Strategic Air Command base in Rapid City, South Dakota.

I want to thank all service members, veterans, and their families again and again for their sacrifices in making our country safe.

CHAPTER 9

Rapid City

O f all places the Air Force could have sent me, they sent me to the same base where my older brother Tom was stationed. The next three and a half years flew by. Rapid City is nestled along the beautiful Black Hills. The weather could easily get above 100 degrees in the summer and 30 degrees below zero in the winter. This western area of South Dakota is a sportsman's paradise. It's also absolutely beautiful.

Ellsworth Air Force Base is 10 miles outside of Rapid City. My job was to guard the powerful Minuteman III Intercontinental Ballistic Missiles, as well as patrol all launch facilities. I was carrying lethal firepower but wasn't old enough to vote. Numerous nuclear missiles in silos were located all across western South Dakota, as well as an alert squadron of the mighty B-52 Stratofortress, completely uploaded, sitting on priority A alert status. Absolutely no one was allowed near them.

I was in awe that I was part of the Strategic Air Command. This was a high-alert security base, and I quickly got a sense of operational readiness for our nation's defense. My job was also to provide security for nuclear convoys and protect the weapons by patrolling much of western South Dakota from a helicopter. Volunteer military security personnel were constantly needed to ride for four-to-six hours at a shot in a fully loaded helicopter piloted by former Vietnam pilots.

It didn't take me long to get back into shape. While driving on patrol, I would talk my partner into letting me get out of the truck and run alongside. I knew that every day would have to count. I joined the Rapid City YMCA and quickly got in with a group of weightlifters. I fit right in, and many of these athletes are still my friends to this day.

Big Tim Callahan took me in. He was a big, gregarious Irishman who made me feel right at home. He encouraged me to join the powerlifting team. We would compete all around the region over the next three years. Tim was like a brother, and I admired him greatly. To provide for his family, he would often have to take on plumbing jobs 600 to 800 miles away. He would always sneak me into the health club at the Y. As soon as my three-day tour of work was done on base, he and I would head for town.

After being in Rapid City for only two weeks, I drove to the YMCA. There was unusual excitement in the weight room. A short young man was squatting more than 600 pounds, full parallel. It was his second world record that day. He couldn't have been more than 5'6" and 150 pounds. Not only that, but he then deadlifted more than 600 pounds for sets of three. I didn't know then that he was the world record holder at the time. I noticed his gym shorts said Jefferson County, the same high school district as mine.

The young man was Ricky Dale Crain, and he was from Arvada West, one of my rival high schools back in Colorado. His parents had moved to Rapid City his senior year of high school. His dad, Don, was the South Dakota powerlifting champion and worked as an accountant on an Indian reservation. Rick had been on a football scholarship but had left college to pursue powerlifting. He would go on to break several world records. In 1977, the U.S. Powerlifting Association rated the top ten powerlifters in the world, and Ricky was number one. I would try to follow every routine he would construct for me.

In 1976, I wanted to do something to honor the bicentennial of our nation. I set out to do 100,000 pushups that year. By the time October rolled around, my body was starting to ache and not recover very well after workouts. This was a severe lesson to learn: don't set crazy goals that fatigue your muscle groups. My triceps were taking a beating, as I was overworking

33

them while competing in national powerlifting tournaments. My bench press also suffered. I learned to set goals that are realistic and safe. The most critical element of exercise might well be recovery.

At the end of my second year in the Air Force, my body was still growing. I was up to 195 pounds. I placed second in the nation at the teenage national powerlifting meet held in El Dorado, Arkansas. I won the South Dakota State Powerlifting Championship. At a big regional meet in Brookings, South Dakota, I placed second out of 17, only losing by a few pounds. I also received the "Outstanding Teenage Lifter" trophy.

By then, I had been in the Air Force three years. This last year would take total dedication. I was 6'0" and weighed 210 pounds. I again won the South Dakota State Powerlifting Championship. I placed fifth the next year at the teenage nationals in Nashua, New Hampshire. The competition there was much tougher, as many young men would drive up from Ohio, Pennsylvania, New Jersey, and surrounding areas.

My younger brother, Ray, was in this competition with me. We both got a firsthand look at anabolic steroid use. We actually saw guys passing pills to each other. We had decided early on that we would only allow our bodies to grow by the "Grace of God" and not through artificial means. This commitment only strengthened our resolve to depend on God, who has always supplied our strength. I won the base powerlifting championship again that year. My friends also talked me into competing in the base power clean competition. Power cleans weren't my favorite competitive lift, but I won the competition anyway, defeating 30 other contestants with a 300 pound effort – 25 pounds more than I had ever lifted before.

A couple of generals and full-bird colonels were present, which had motivated me. Both generals were Vietnam veterans. After I received my trophy, I was headed to my car when something came over me. I returned to the pavilion. I asked for the bar to be loaded back up to 315 pounds, then I let out a scream and lifted the weight easier than the 300 pounds only a few minutes earlier. To have a 2 and 3 star generals embrace me was all I needed for encouragement.

I felt like I was on target for my collegiate goal, as I only had a little over a year to go on my enlistment. Since high school, I had grown a couple of inches and gained over 60 pounds.

During my last year in the military, my good friend Don Harris and I moved off base. We found a house in downtown Rapid City, much closer to the YMCA. Don was a disciplined bodybuilder, and we motivated each other. I finally got my bench press to 405 pounds, my squat to 500 pounds, my power clean to 280 for five reps, and my dead lift to 570 pounds. Rapid City was a great area for running, as it had trails all over town. I often did sprints at the Western Dakota Technical Institute track in town.

In the dead of winter, I arrived in Brookings, South Dakota, for a huge regional powerlifting meet. I had a restless night sleeping in a dorm that was way too hot. The meet lasted for more than seven hours, and we were all exhausted. We should have stayed in a hotel that night but instead decided to start the 400-mile drive home at midnight. I put in my Michael Murphy 8-track and lasted until about five in the morning. I had just driven 330 miles and couldn't stay awake any longer. Big George took the wheel for the last 100 miles. I fell into a deep sleep.

It wasn't 30 minutes later when I felt our van swerving off the road into the middle of the interstate. Big George, recently back from a base in Thailand, had fallen asleep at the wheel. He had almost got us back on the highway when the van drove over a huge metal pipe, ripping one of our back tires completely off. The van then slid back across the highway onto its side and started to roll off the other side of the highway down to the bottom of the hill. As the van rolled the first five times, I was able to keep cart wheeling inside. By the last two rolls, I couldn't keep up.

As the van stopped rolling, I slowly started to move and heard the other two passengers moving around, which let me know they were alive. Mike was on the back floor of the van moaning. His head was wedged under the back door. I knew I had to free him, as he could drown in his own blood. I was able to pry the back doors open, freeing Mike's head, which had been split wide open. I knew that you're not supposed to move an injured body, but it was 10 degrees above zero, and I had to keep him warm. I pulled a mattress from the van, set it on the ground, and laid his body on top. I then covered him up with a blanket and jacket. George was out cold in the driver's seat with his head smashed into the windshield. I pulled him back to a reclined position and wiped the blood off his face. I then limped up to the highway to flag down a motorist.

Our Good Samaritan drove a semi. The driver met me on the highway with a first aid kit. He helped apply direct pressure to the left side of my head and then made me lay down on the interstate as he radioed for help. He covered my feet with his jacket; I didn't even know that I was barefoot. Next, I felt a warm sensation, and several medical people hovered over me. After several hours at the hospital, George and I were released to military personnel, who transported us back to base. We had to leave Mike at the hospital, where he would receive more than 160 stitches. His parents came to pick him up.

We had totaled Ricky Dale Crain's van. He hadn't been at the meet, but he had allowed us to borrow it. Unfortunately, we were only able to return his set of keys. Sorry, Ricky! I was sore and unable to lift for the next two weeks. My head was pretty soft and bruised (many think it still is). My knee was sore, and

I had several cuts. Big George was back working out with us three weeks later. We were all grateful to be alive.

One Saturday morning, we flew in from a tour of duty. The pilot asked me if I was going to the arm wrestling championship just off base in the town of Box Elder. Still in my uniform, I drove off base and stopped in at the bar where the event was being held. To my surprise, many of my local YMCA friends had entered. I thought I would stick around to see how they would do. Before I knew it, my friends had entered me in the contest.

My first match was against a large dude off a ranch in Huron, South Dakota. I put him down with the greatest of ease, along with the next guy and the next. I beat some of my closest friends who had arm wrestled for years, and in less than an hour I was up for the championship prize money. As the referee positioned our hands for the final match, I winked at all my friends. They thought I was nuts. In less than two seconds, I put a big Minnesota plumber down on his side. I won 200 dollars, reimbursed the guys for the entry fee, and said goodbye. I don't think that went over so well, as they had all trained hard for the contest. Some friends and I went off to enjoy the great, historic town of Deadwood.

The Black Hills was also the home of the quaint little town of Sturgis, South Dakota. My patrol area took me through this town every tour of duty. I never knew what all the fuss was about until I saw it with my own eyes. While on patrol one August night we got a code 1 radio alert telling all military personnel to avoid Sturgis at all costs.

There were reports of live cattle rustling. I just had to see it with my own eyes. Since I was in charge of my patrol, I told my B man that today was opposite day – we had been instructed to stay away, which meant we had to go see what was happening. It was a little past dark, around nine p.m., when we drove into Sturgis. My partner and I just about flipped out as we pulled into town and saw flames rising high into the Dakota sky. A gigantic cow was high off the ground on a homemade spit with several bikers rotating it over the fire. It was the most fantastic thing I ever witnessed in the Black Hills. Nobody would believe our story until they read it in the paper the following day.

We parked there for more than two hours, watching bikers ride round and round in circles, often driving through the fire. I wanted to leave the truck to join them, but I couldn't since I was in uniform and concealing lots of firepower in our truck.

CHAPTER 10

Ready to Deal

———————❖———————

I had only a few months left on my tour of duty in Rapid City. A big, solid dude named Bob Geddes came down to the YMCA early one Saturday morning looking for bouncers for the big Black Hills Music Fest of 1979. He was former Denver Bronco linebacker and in charge of security. "I need 10 guys ready to deal," he said.

I personally assured him that I could supply 10 well-qualified meat eaters for the big event, just one week away. The headliners included Fleetwood Mac, Heart, Willie Nelson, Waylon Jennings, Jessi Coulter, The Outlaws, Kris Kristofferson, Jim Dandy, Bob Welch, and Crystal Gayle.

During the concert, my nine best friends and I pretty much had the green light to secure the performers, the stage, the back-stage, and all of the grounds. It was on! Within the first 10 minutes, two dudes tried to rush the stage only to be met with severe resistance. We literally sent them flying back into the crowd. This continued for hours. I launched at least 15 people off stage, and we pounded another 10 trying to break in to the performer's dressing room.

By the day's end, we were exhausted. When Bob had said we needed to be ready to deal, he hadn't been joking. I was the leading tackler once again, especially trying to keep people off of Willie Nelson. You should have seen my gang trying to keep the scavengers away from Stevie Nicks and Christine McVie. It was like the "bull in the ring" football drill – we would put one of the trespassers in the middle of the circle and focus on using good technique in tackling and forearm smashes. Many of the rowdies would try to climb the flagpole. We kept them off and protected the performers at all costs. This battle royale would go on all day long.

At the end of the day, we received our second free meal, a tee shirt, $80 in cash, and the fine compliment, "You were ready to deal!" All the members of Fleetwood Mac thanked us, and Bob Welch thanked me personally. Waylon Jennings and Willie Nelson gave us all a thumbs up. Jessi Coulter gave me a hug, and I didn't want to let her go. Ann and Nancy Wilson gave out free kisses and asked if I was going to protect them at their next show in Chicago.

We all went home exhausted after having the time of our lives. We would talk about this concert for years to come.

CHAPTER 11

The Big Red Caravan

here I was in the middle of South Dakota, not far from the Badlands. It was a bright, sunny morning, and I had just been digging our military truck out of the mud on a missile site. After several hours of exhausting work, I looked to the highway only to see a long caravan of red vehicles, many of them Cadillacs. What exactly was this strange parade heading west on I-90? I drove out to the service road and could hardly believe my eyes. I had never seen nor heard of such a spectacle. As I drew closer, I could see signs of "Go Big Red!" A lot of the vehicles had an "N" on them. Did the "N" stand for Nebraska? I had to call my brother Ray in Denver. Could all these people be traveling in support of Nebraska's football team?

This was quite a following. I had never imagined so much support for any team at any level! I had to admit that it got me fired up for college football. I would never forget what I saw that morning. They must have been heading to play Wyoming, Montana, or maybe Washington in a pre-season tilt somewhere out west. All I could do was take off my Air Force uniform shirt and then the University of Colorado football tee shirt I was wearing underneath. There I was standing out on the interstate waving my CU football tee shirt at the passersby. Many people in the vehicles gave me the bird of paradise. I was hoping they might all take a left at Mount Rushmore, get lost in the Badlands, and have to sleep on the ground, especially the week they would be playing Colorado!

I knew had to make each workout count. I couldn't wait to get back to the base and work out, but first a triple scoop of chocolate ice cream from the famous Wall Drug.

Chapter 12

Brother Ray

———————————❧———————————

My younger brother, Ray, was graduating from high school just as I was finishing the Air Force. He was 6'2" and around 215 pounds. I had sent him routines, power-lifting equipment, and tee shirts from every meet I had entered over the past four years. He was an all-state football player and averaged about 20 points per game in basketball, yet baseball may have been his first love. He would bat clean-up and hit line drives out of the park. Powerlifting was also a passion of his, and he was the state high school powerlifting champion. He had a 605 pound dead lift, which is still a high school record in Colorado for his weight class. I don't know how he did it.

Unlike me, Ray had two full drawers of letters and packets from Division One colleges. One day a recruiter from Notre Dame came to Jefferson High wearing his prestigious green jacket and looking for Ray Cone. The entire school beamed with excitement, proud to see the mighty fighting Irish in the house. One day, LaVell Edwards, BYU's head coach, was in our living room. My parents would have loved for Ray to play for him, as he was such a wonderful gentleman. Oregon State, Texas, UCLA, Arizona, Wyoming, Colorado State, SMU, and Oregon all worked hard to get him to sign with their teams. More than one had a serious offer for him – cars, jobs, clothing, and a private plane to take the parents to the games.

Ray had a different style of running. Many times while carrying the ball, he would break into the open. Then instead of running straight for the goal line, he would stray to the right or to the left to find somebody to hit. Not only was Ray a hard nose runner, he was a punishing linebacker. With his face painted blazing red before the start of a game against Golden High School, he had run over to the visiting team's locker room, kicked in the door, and stepped inside screaming, "I'm going to kick your ass!" Then he had taken a swing at an empty bench and knocked it out of the wall. Years later, Golden's head coach, Bob Stickline, admitted that Ray had scared several of his players and coaches as that bench fell to the ground.

During this recruiting frenzy, I always hoped that Ray would choose the University of Colorado. I remember Ray praying about his decision. In the end, he said goodbye to basketball and baseball, and he was on his way with a full-ride football scholarship to the University of Colorado.

CHAPTER 13

Welcome to the
University of Colorado Boulder

T hen came my turn. After four long years of prepara-
tion and heavy training, I was finally in Boulder. I still
believe this is the most beautiful setting for a campus anywhere
in the United States. The Flatirons offer a gorgeous, pristine
backdrop to the city of Boulder. The campus itself is a sight to
behold. As many coaches, professors, and students have said,
"Boulder can recruit itself." And it's true. Students immediately
fall in love with everything they see.

During my next four years in Boulder, I would be in an
athletic training Mecca. There were possibly more Olympic
athletes in training there than in any other city in the United
States. The mile-high altitude (5,430 feet) made Boulder ideal
for training.

We would often see a human flash running across the campus at an extremely high rate of speed. I recognized the runner instantly. It was Frank Shorter, the 1972 U.S. gold medalist in the marathon. He ran 26.2 miles in a little over two hours. He was also the 1976 silver medalist in the same event, running the entire distance only to lose the gold by 30 seconds. Whenever I would see him race across campus, I would yell out, "Frank Shorter, remember 72." He would always wave at me.

The top U.S. steeplechasers and runners were constantly training in and around campus, and Olympic cycling teams were constantly weaving in and out of traffic. Many international athletes took classes in the physical education and exercise physiology department. One dude named Gary had just finished running an ultra-marathon (more than 400 miles) in a little over five days. We would always see him in the library hanging out with the track athletes. I remember him telling his friends that his goal was to run 100 miles the very first day of the marathon – then the rest would be easy. In my psychology classes, our professor, Dr. Dave Wardell, would often bring top Olympic athletes to speak to our class. Needless to say, Dr. Wardell always had the most popular class on campus.

In 1982, Professor Denny, the religious studies department head and a wonderful professor, asked our class to guess how many religions there were in Boulder. After careful thought, I guessed 40. Another dude from the back guessed 60. The professor told us we were way off. The answer was more than 300! Boulder may be one of the true cultural centers of the universe. Back in the 70s, Boulder was one of the major homes of the hippie movement. People had a saying in Boulder: "How do you get to Berkeley? Simple: you go to Boulder and take a left!" All this diversity in such a beautiful setting is what makes Boulder, Colorado, one of the most intriguing cities in the world.

I felt deep inside that I could fit in. The military had been real good to me. I had gained close to 80 pounds since high school, and each year I was slowly raising the bar on my personal best in all weightlifting categories. Denver's East High School had just hosted the Rocky Mountain Powerlifting Championships. I was fortunate enough to win my weight class and blow away several competitors in the bench press, parallel squat, and dead lift. I had once competed against some of these dudes back in high school. It was great to be home in Denver.

During my four years in the military, I had grown up and seen more of the world. I had gained decision-making skills and a sense of confidence. I had learned to break the tie to my parents, continuing to value their opinion without depending on them to tell me what to do. I learned how to motivate myself. And I gained a much stronger appreciation for my family, friends, and country.

Chapter 14

Bracket Hall

I was getting a little nervous, as I had to find lodging. Thank goodness one room was available in the football dorm, Brackett Hall. As a walk-on, there are no guarantees, not even a place to stay. I was fortunate – I could have been living downtown, in an off-campus apartment, or at home 20 miles away. Finally I was in the athletic dorm, eating, sleeping, and living in an all-football environment. I wondered if I was really the newest member of this Golden Buffaloes program or if I was dreaming. Over the last four years, not a day had gone by without my dreaming of this experience. Trophies, jerseys, and pictures adorned the walls of this hallowed institution and captivated my mind and spirit.

Such a wide variety of athletes filled these rooms, some small, some medium, but mostly big. There were linemen ready to enter the NFL draft and tight ends ready to enter the first round. The skilled positions were full of sleek, muscular, and hard-nose players, athletes from all over the country who had won at any sport they had ever played. Some were blue chip all Americans, selecting Boulder over many other top-ranked programs. This wasn't high school. To stand out here, I would have to strap it on.

Living here amongst my teammates put me at an all-time high. Just to be there, as part of this brotherhood, motivated me beyond my wildest dreams. I felt that I could fit right in. This is what I had worked so hard for. I don't believe anybody was more pumped up than I was. At night I would sneak out across the street down into Folsom Stadium and run as long as I could. I would be under the stars, the heavens, the lights of Boulder, with the entire stadium all to myself. I would dream of 60,000 people filling the arena.

Often around 10 p.m. hunger made its final curtain call. The halls reminded me of *The Night of the Living Dead*, with hungry, tired athletic zombies combing the halls. A quick call to Domino's would do the trick, and usually within 30 minutes or less our hunger was satisfied. Once a pizza was delivered, if it made it to the room that is, the door was immediately locked, and the feast began. My biggest concern was when three extra-large pizzas were delivered to only three players. Imagine the calorie fest taking place.

Word had it that as the late-night rounds of pizza were delivered, the trees and bushes around Brackett Hall would come to life. In the shroud of darkness, a lean, starving athlete would appear. Within seconds, the delivery man would be tossed to the ground, his coin purse plundered, and the pizza taken. According to the campus newspaper, Domino's rated Brackett Hall as the most dangerous delivery destination of all of the nation's campuses. The 911 calls were becoming all too familiar to campus police. One cold night, I gazed out my third-story window only to hear several sirens off in the distance. I could see the emergency vehicles coming closer and closer until they pulled up in front of our dorm. I went downstairs, and sure enough another Domino's driver had been thrown down and out on the pavement. After several more altercations, we were informed that Domino's would no longer deliver. Brackett Hall was off limits.

My next door neighbors were both 7'1" basketball players. At the semester break, one of them transferred back east. The new roommate, Curtis, was from Chicago, standing 5'10". Curtis and Cooper would walk around campus together all the time. They were almost 15 inches different in height.

In the spring, Curtis brought back his 750 Honda motorcycle from Chicago. One of his neighbors growing up was Isaiah Thomas, and now they could ride all over Boulder together. It was hilarious. Whenever Curtis would be driving, he wouldn't put his feet down at the stoplights. Big Cooper would lower his feet down to the ground while sitting in back and hold the bike up whenever they came to a stop. It was a sight to behold.

Counting the garden level, Bracket Hall had three levels. My room was high up on the third floor facing the north. A huge tree sat just outside the window. A strong branch could be easily accessed just by removing the screen and stepping onto it. In came Luke from McDonald, Pennsylvania. With curly red hair and a great sense of humor, Luke was easily welcomed into our group. I noticed Luke gazing out to the north at our wonderful tree. I removed the screen and climbed out on the branch. Luke thought it was pretty cool, so when I came back in I suggested he give it a try.

Luke climbed out on the limb, making monkey noises and rocking back and forth over students passing under on the way to class. I secretly locked the window and called campus police and said that we had a possible jumper up in the tree in front of Brackett Hall. By this time, quite a crowd of people had gathered to look up and laugh at Luke.

From a distance, I could see police units rolling up to our dorm. I ran out and told them that I thought he may jump as he seemed unstable. Four officers circled the tree, telling him to come down. Luke told the cops it was all a practical joke. The campus police questioned him and determined he could return to dorm life. Luke was a funny guy, and I think they logged the funny guy's name just in case he pulled any other stunts.

One day, word surfaced that a 6'10" basketball star had stolen one of the coach's credit cards and was using it to call countries all over the world just for kicks. He called Germany, Australia, England, Japan, the Philippines, and Indonesia. This went on for a couple of weeks until he started calling his mom. That was the end of his calling spree, as they easily traced the calls. He had to leave campus that next semester. It was too bad since he had been an outstanding player. Back in high school in Michigan, he had once blocked 25 shots, stunning the Friday night crowds. He also may have been the sweetest guy on CU's basketball team.

CHAPTER 15

Mark Bergdale

W hen you think of Brackett Hall, you can't help but think of Mark Bergdale. He lived in the apartment on the main floor of our football dorm. By day he was an English professor, afternoons he would help coach us, and at night he would patrol the halls until all was calm. Mark was a former athlete from Gettysburg College in Pennsylvania. He was 6'2" and weighed about 225 pounds. He had been an outstanding collegiate wrestler as well. With long blonde hair to his shoulders, he looked like a Viking.

To get Mark's attention, all we would have to do was light a firecracker, scream, or beat on the pipes around 11 p.m. during his rounds, and he would be at our doom room within minutes. We would leave our door slightly open, and the second he would arrive I would leap off my upper bunk onto this back.

The fight was on! Our bouts would last anywhere from 10 to 15 minutes. He was one tough, hard-nosed wrestler.

As Mark made his nightly rounds, I would sometimes be lurking in the laundry room or utility room or jump out from behind the shower curtain. These matches definitely built strength and endurance! If a few days would go by and my scouts hadn't seen Mark, I would take the fight to him. A light knock on his door was all it would take. "Who is it?" Mark would ask, and in a high-pitched voice I would reply, "I need your help!" The second his door was open, down to the ground we would go.

He really helped out with our studies. Many people felt that Mark Bergdale taught the Cone brothers how to speak, read, and write. We learned that Mark had taught an entire class back east while standing on his head. I've never seen a person walk so fast across campus in my life. My brother and I would have to jog to keep up with him. He was all business, never slowing down enough to notice the babes checking him out.

Mark was good-natured, a great friend, and like a big brother. Thank you, Mark.

CHAPTER 16

The Eye in the Sky

Every player in college football has heard of the Eye in the Sky. It's a network of cameras filming every phase of practice. That's right, players are always being watched. Not only will these films help players improve, they'll also find players out. The film crew can zoom in on your position, so if you're a little on the lazy side, you'll be exposed. The coaches literally spend hours studying and breaking down films. These coaches are geniuses who can figure out exactly who you are in four plays or less. Some coaches can figure you out just by watching you stand around. We weren't in high school anymore.

Let this be a warning to all. Make a commitment from your earliest playing days to work as hard as you can, whenever you can. It will pay off, and you will be noticed! Remember, all this hard work and commitment will be your legacy. It helps to define your character. We all know guys who slack off, try to get out of workouts, and take the easy way out. Remember what the former Oklahoma Sooner and Congressman J.C. Watts says: "Character is doing the right thing when nobody is looking!" J.C. should know about character and commitment, as he would always torment the Colorado Buffalos every time he played against them. He was a one-man wrecking crew.

The Eye in the Sky is a great learning tool. Use it for your betterment.

CHAPTER 17

Meat Squad

W hat a class act this Big Eight football program was. I was awestruck with Coach Chuck Fairbanks running the show. He had taken the New England Patriots from worst to first. His legend still lives on at the University of Oklahoma. Once I was in pads I actually felt bulletproof. I could hardly wait to do battle. Bart Roth, a former standout linebacker at CU, was my mentor as inside linebacker. He would patiently stand over me, and say, "Stay low and read your keys and avenue of pursuits." I can never thank him enough.

It suddenly dawned on me that I was an inside linebacker going against a starting Big Eight offense. We were to replicate the upcoming defense Colorado would face every Saturday. Coach Fairbanks would always say, "Give us a good look, please." This scout team would become my life. Other scout team members were just there, not giving much effort. Not me. I was really hungry, maybe because I had been away for four years. I was there because I craved it! I had an insatiable thirst for full contact. I declared war on anybody who would come near me. I would do anything the coaches would ask. It's all about making the team better – it's not all about you!

As I walked around campus, I would always see fellow players, which authenticated my joy and love for the game. It was a true privilege to be a part of such a great group of guys. I would develop new friends for life.

Coach Fairbanks was a true technician. Sometimes he would run over my gap six times in a row just to get a play right. I would live for the compliment of "Who didn't block him?" or "Where did he come in from to mess up our play?" Every practice was filmed for the entire coaching staff to see. I would totally give it my all, and this staff would give us the red carpet treatment. Everything was first class. With a new locker room, a weight room, and steak night twice a week at the dining hall, life wasn't too bad. If you work yourself half to death and find yourself on the meat squad, consider it a reward. (Call it the "scout team" if you want, but for me "meat squad" is just fine.) This is the place where you can establish yourself. It's where you can earn the respect of your teammates and coaches. Just remember, it takes each individual to make a team better. When you walk off the field after Saturday's game, it's gratifying to know you're a part of it. This meat squad was my ticket to being placed on all special teams, which also meant the traveling squad.

The biggest surprise to me was being under the influence of a former NFL coaching staff. Coach Fairbanks as well as most of his staff had coached at a top collegiate level or in the pro ranks. Everything was run on a pro format. I was pretty much in awe. I couldn't believe that across from me stood an offensive lineman at 6'5" and 280 pounds. The tight end was a preseason All-American before his sophomore year. The guards were low to the ground and the best of the best. The center would be high in the NFL draft the very next year. It was truly an honor to be a part of this team. I gave thanks every day I entered and left the field.

CHAPTER 18

Not So Fast

T here must be discipline in weight training. Many athletes feel that practice and the games keep them in sufficient shape, but that isn't always the case. It's hard, very hard to lift weights after practice or during the season. Your body is bruised, and your joints usually ache, plus you're exhausted after being on the field for a demanding three-hour practice. You're starving and thirsty. This is where most athletes lose valuable strength. I would pay attention to how much a player could bench press before the season started because the amount would usually decrease during the season by 30 to 40 pounds. After the season and a short time off, the players would begin the strength rebuilding process. It would take weeks to regain the weight they were once lifting.

If you hustle, just after practice you can grab two or three of your disciplined friends and head directly to the weight room.

While in high school, you can lift during the season in PE class, but in college it's not so easy. You have to make your own time. Most players remove their tape, hang out, goof off, and then shower up before they dash off to the dining hall. If you proceed to the weight room directly after practice, the benefits are enormous. You need to pick four of your favorite lifts and do at least six sets of each. Try to set a goal of 30 to 40 minutes at least three times per week. All four years, no more than six or eight players ever worked out after practice. My brother Ray was my lifting partner. On these quicker, abbreviated workouts, we would do bench presses, military presses, upright rows, triceps and bicep curls for the girls! In this way, we were able to sustain our strength throughout the season.

The best program we ever used was five sets of five on the bench press. You started with 80 to 100 pounds below your max when two-a-day practices started. Then you did bench presses on Mondays and Fridays, adding five pounds per week. With perseverance and patience, at the end of 12 weeks you'd be doing five sets of five with an amount that you had never bench pressed before. Then the next time you started the routine, you started your five sets of five with 10 or 15 pounds more than you had started with before. By the time you were finished, only 30 or 35 minutes would have gone by. You really needed to increase your intensity. You couldn't drag your workout beyond this time. You needed to push each other the whole time because you were already tired. On middle day of the week, you did everything except bench press.

By the time you got to the locker room, most guys were gone. It was nice because there weren't big crowds in your way. And you got to the dining hall in perfect time with the line just about gone.

Each Monday, Wednesday, and Friday night was also pushup night. I would do 250 to 300 each. Tuesday and Thursday nights were our heavy chin-up workout (70-80 reps) in the third-story bathroom, where a chin-up bar had been hung over an abandoned shower stall. Remember, as a walk on you weren't considered equal to the player next to you. You had to be driven, and you had to excel. Nobody was begging you to stay, work out, or even be there. I had thought high school was fun, even the military, but my long-awaited dream to play college football meant there was much more at stake. It was more serious, and everything counted, so I often thought twice before I ate or relaxed.

This goes for any athlete who has set a goal. As you get older, you get tired much easier. After dinner, the second you hit the couch it's over. You need to just go for it! A quick 20-minute workout at least three to four times per week will work wonders.

CHAPTER 19

Hitting the Books

I wasn't exactly a stranger to classwork, as I had taken 15 hours of night classes during my four years in the Air Force. In Boulder I was ready to study. I took 15 hours my first semester at Boulder, and I was blessed to have two pre-med players as roommates, which was important for my college survival. One of them, Dave, was possibly the most disciplined student athlete I had ever met. (He would later become a prominent chiropractor.) He would rewrite his class notes daily and wear out his welcome at the professor's office hours weekly. He had schedules, formulas, and notes neatly taped to his wall. I don't know if Dave ever got less than an A. He was a devout Christian, and he didn't like to party or partake in any unnatural or foreign herb. He had attended Pomona High School in Arvada, Colorado, and had been one of the top decathletes in the state.

He was a transfer student from the University of Wyoming and had perhaps the finest pair of hands for a tight end that I had ever seen. I picked up some fine study habits from him.

Some of my classes had more than 400 students. Many times I'd see most of those students the first day, midterm day, and for the final. My major was to be exercise physiology, and I took enough hours to have a minor in history, religious studies, and geography. I loved to learn, possibly because I had had so much time away from studies. To succeed, I had to be disciplined, as I was exhausted most of the time. I was tied up with football for more than 40 hours per week. I had a meeting every day at one p.m., and then I had to get my ankles taped and practice at three p.m. Off to the field till around six p.m., workout, shower, dinner, and done by around eight. Then I had to find the strength to study. It was all good but very demanding. I had to keep above a C average or I would be ineligible to play. It was time to become a young man. I wanted to make my parents proud. Some classes tested my moral beliefs and values, but I stayed strong, and tried to uphold godly values. I learned that if you make a decision to commit yourself to excellence, excellence will become part of your character.

CHAPTER 20

First Collegiate Game

W e were all coached up and ready to go. I think I woke up six times that night. The Harvest House Hotel provided us with a nice room and a huge breakfast. The state patrol, sirens blaring, led us safely to campus. Then we went into the locker room to be taped and get dressed. Those three hours before the game flew by. All players walked around firing each other up. We trotted onto the field, ready for our pre-game warm-ups.

Oh how I had longed for this day. Pristine skies over Boulder, brand-new shoes and uniforms, the marching band warming up, the Boulder turnpike packed, traffic jams all the way back to Denver, parking lots filled with tailgaters, and all of our families showing up. It was priceless! People headed down from Wyoming, Fort Collins, Pueblo, and all over the region. People poured in from almost every city and county in Colorado to support our team. The stadium was already about 80 percent full.

The pageantry of college football is beyond words. In comes your opponent with 55 buffed players looking to knock you out. Back home every one of them had been a high school star. Friends come to the side rail to give high fives and take a quick picture. The marching band warms up. Kim, the girl out in the middle of our field twirling her baton, is a former Ms. Colorado. Out walks an impressive crew of Big Eight officials who ask every player to reveal any hidden casts or questionable padding.

Players are constantly looking to the stands to see if their family has arrived. Girlfriends show up with friends in tow. All your emotions and physical strength are geared toward this moment. Larry Zimmer and Bobby Anderson, the voices of the Buffs, were already broadcasting the pregame show on radio 850. My dream was to have them call my name over the loudspeakers just like my high school days.

I think I was running on pure adrenalin. How cool to see everyone from little kids to grownups all sporting the black and gold. Hamburgers and hot dogs filled the air with a pleasing aroma. People yelled out the players' names. It was heaven on earth.

I would be starting on all special teams this day, as I was a backup linebacker somewhere down the list. I was focused on the task at hand. The staff believed in me enough to put me on all the special teams. I wasn't about to let any of them down.

After our pregame stretch and drills, we regrouped in the tunnel and followed Ralphie, the Buffalo mascot, onto the field. I was always glad to get off the field after pregame drills because players were so pumped up that we almost killed each other before the game ever started. Players were so amped that we were crushing each other. After "The Star Spangled Banner" played, I could hardly breathe. My legs felt heavy. I felt butterflies in my stomach.

I heard "Colorado elects to kick off, kickoff team get ready!" Within a moment I was on the field for first time in more than four years. My dream had just come to fruition. Now if I could only get my legs to respond and my brain to stay sharp and focused, I would be alright. I waved to my folks on the 40 yard line, 26 rows high. My uncles, friends, workout partners, old teachers, and coaches were all present. I literally knew people all over the stadium. The game was being broadcast all over the region.

As the kick sailed high in the mile-high air, it was caught on the goal line. Out came the ball carrier at a high rate of speed. I sprinted down the field as fast as my 6'0", 222-pound frame would take me. I was hit hard from the left and had barely regained my balance when I was blindsided from the right. I was knocked directly into the ball carrier for my first-ever collegiate solo tackle. Over the loudspeaker, I heard, "#45, Marty Cone on the tackle." A solo tackle as my first collegiate play – I was beside myself! I ran to the sideline just about out of my mind and definitely out of breath.

Then there was the punt team. I was on it, positioned right next to my brother Ray, #49. We would sprint down as hard as we could and sandwich the unsuspecting blocker or ball carrier. Special teams are a blast! If you're placed on them, consider yourself blessed. You'll sprint, block, and tackle all game long until you're exhausted. It's a real privilege. Oftentimes you'll have the chance to draw the "first blood." This entire game was my crowning jewel.

Punt return was perhaps the ultimate. To start the play, I would quickly lunge and knock the long snapper to the ground, then circle back to form the wall. If I hustled, I could knock down one or two more players. I had more than 10 knockdowns that very first game. Kickoff returns were as fun as the punt returns. Guys would run down the field at full speed. You can catch them just as they turn and blindside them, sending them sailing to the turf. I was so stoked playing special teams that all I could do was thank the coaches every day. I would run until the whistle blew, whereas many players gave one good surge and that was it. I believe you can bash an extra 10 or 15 players a game if you sprint to the whistle. I would try to hit those players so hard that their mom could feel it.

These games will have you talking for days. My brother and I would tell of the body count we would leave behind. You see, Ray had a mean streak, and if he was on the field you knew someone was going to get thumped! We were comrades in arms. What a blast, what a life. We would talk for hours and take in everybody's account of what had happened. This game went down as the most exciting sports moments of my life.

Everyone you face will be on scholarship, and all of them will be looking to light you up. Other players want to see a big hit on their game film as well. Train hard. You'll make memories that you won't forget the rest of your life.

Chapter 21

UCLA Road Trip

———————✦———————

I made the traveling squad. I could hardly believe it. We would be taking on the mighty UCLA Bruins, loaded with talent, and we would be staying at a five-star hotel in LA, a real first-class trip. After we touched down at LAX, we got on the team bus en route to the City of Angels. That year we had several players from the LA area. It didn't take long for one of them to start bragging about his LA exploits, saying, "Man, on that corner right there is where I beat up two dudes." The next guy said, "Man, on that corner is where I fell in love." Another said, "Man, on that corner is where my baby proposed to me," and yet another said, "Man on that football field over there I ran for 350 yards." This went on for hours – it was hilarious! I didn't know we had so many legends on one bus.

We finally made it to the field at the Los Angeles Coliseum, where Roman Gabriel, Merlin Olson, Deacon Jones, and the

Rams used to play. It was a beautiful 70-degree day in Southern California, the breathtaking San Gabriel Mountains off to the east and the Pacific Ocean to the west. I looked over to the stands. I saw three old high school friends out from Colorado for the game. I managed to sneak over and say hello.

UCLA had an outstanding team that year. The Bruins had a slender quarterback on the sidelines, Rich Neuheisal, who would later become Colorado's head coach. He was good looking with locks of golden hair like a surfer dude and a big crowd around him. I couldn't believe the depth of talent three and four rows deep on UCLA's sideline. I think our entire team was a little nervous. I watched closely as their wide receivers ran pass patterns before the game. One sleek, lightning-fast wide-out was Karl Dorrell, who would later become UCLA's head coach, only to be replaced by Rick Neuheisal.

On the kickoff return, I was on the front wall. I had worked out a plan for our deep back, Walter Stanley (Green Bay Packers). I told him where to run back on the kickoffs so we could create a small opening between myself and the front wall blocker next to me. I would take my guy to the left; the guy blocking next to me would take his man to the right. It was such a blast. We would open a narrow avenue, and suddenly we could hear players coming up behind us. Sure enough, it would be Walter. We had seven or eight chances and got the ball out to the 40 yard line or better. We fought hard, and though we fell short Walter was leading the nation in kickoff return yardage by the end of the game.

While in LA, I got to watch the best defensive player I ever played against, Kenny Easley #45. He was the strong safety for UCLA, a one-man wrecking crew. Many of us players were in awe of how he singlehandedly destroyed us. None of us could stop him. I wouldn't dare ask him to take off my number, #45.

LA was also the home of Derek Singleton, our starting running back. He was a wonderful athlete who chose Colorado over many California schools. We admired his work ethic and his friendship. He was only with us a short time, however, as he contracted meningitis and died during the season. It was a great loss, and we all were in tears. Our thoughts and prayers went out to his family. I had a chance to hug his parents at the memorial. It was a real privilege to know him. We were all proud of Coach Fairbanks, as he handled the whole situation with dignity and class.

Los Angeles is beautiful. With the ocean, palm trees, a light haze, and wonderful mountains, people out there have it made. It was a fantastic road trip! I did, however, learn a lesson on patience. Two linebackers went down due to injuries, and I thought I would be the next backer in, yet I was passed over. I couldn't believe it. It took me awhile to figure out that the player who was put in was a freshman on a full-ride scholarship, whereas I was a walk-on. I knew I was better than that player. Two choices came to mind: Sulk or increase focus and continue to improve. I chose the higher road.

CHAPTER 22

Arnold's Diet Part 1

The University of Colorado basketball manager, Arnold, was our dear friend. He was from Phoenix, Arizona, where he had attended prestigious Brophy College Prep. He even owned a show horse and would compete in events when he was back home. He lived in Bracket Hall just two doors down from me. He would always come down to my room and hang out. He was a classy guy. He wore clothing that I had never heard of, Izod, Polo, Halston, Gucci, and Sperry to name a few. I always wondered why he would need four or five pairs of top-siders.

Arnold stopped in as I was doing sit-ups late one night. He was tired of being unhappy, overweight, and out of shape. He asked me to set him up a program to help him lose at least 30 pounds. He may have been around 5'9" and 220 pounds, so for Arnold it was on! Arnold started watching his diet and doing sit-ups every night, and pretty soon the pounds flew off. My brother and I would be in his room at 9 p.m. for 300 to 400 sit-ups. Now for the first time he was making smart food choices and eating many more salads in the dining hall. Sometimes late at night my bro and I would go down to his room just to rough him up and welcome him to the Big Eight.

About six weeks later, Arnold popped in my room. "I did it, I lost 30 pounds!" he said. We were all so happy for him. Arnold then called my brother and me down to his room for a private meeting. He opened his closet door and said, "Would you guys like any of these clothes? They'll never fit me again." We each walked away with close to 10 shirts a piece, and I got an extra four or five pairs of jeans. The pants wouldn't fit my brother, as he had now moved to offensive guard, and his butt was way too big.

We would wear these clothes for the next three years and become two of the best-dressed players on campus. Thanks again, Arnold!

CHAPTER 23

Roadside Blessing

Early one morning Assistant Coach Hubbard needed two players to help move around 50 boxes from one office to another in north Boulder. He would always ask me first on all special occasions. The pay was $40. My brother and I were out the door in a flash, as we could use the money. The work took us nearly five hours, but we got a free lunch. We finished around 1 p.m. and had to hustle back to campus for 3 p.m. practice.

On the way back, we stopped at a red light up on the diagonal highway. We looked over on the side of the road and saw a man in dire straits. He was leaning against a stop sign and really hurting. It looked like he had been abandoned and left to die, so we pulled off the road to see if we could help. His face had been badly sunburned, and his lips were severely cracked and dry. The shirt on his back was down to strips of cloth, his pants soiled and torn. Long strands of blonde hair covered much of his face. We were without words. We quickly gave him all the water we had left.

I was wearing my brand-new reversible blue and red gym shirt. I took it off and helped him put it on. My brand-new Levi jeans were close to his size, perhaps a little loose, so off they went. My brother gave up his new Nike tennis shoes and his tee shirt. Then we each gave the man $20 from our day's work. We also gave him a small Bible and prayed with him, asking Almighty God to protect him. We felt it was time for us to bless someone as God had blessed us.

Back at campus we had to scurry to our dorm. I was only in my underwear with my jacket wrapped around my waist. Ray was in his socks and shirtless. We made it to practice with only a few moments to spare. That night we went down the hall looking for our friend Jay Humphries (Milwaukee Bucks). He appreciated what we had done and gave Ray two pairs of Converse All-Stars, which fit Ray just fine. Thanks, Jay!

Chapter 24

Buck Teeth

Carl "Buck" Nystrom was our offensive line coach. He had been brought in from Michigan by Coach Fairbanks. Coach Buck was considered the best offensive line coach in the country. He was rugged, tough, mean, nasty, and not afraid to jump in and rip someone's head off. I considered him a friend and had lots of respect for him.

One day, I went into his offensive line meeting room where he was teaching. The season was dragging on a bit, and I felt that the team needed a little jumpstart before practice. I skirted behind the coach and saw his dentures sitting on the rail at the chalkboard that holds the erasers. His dentures had three teeth, old tobacco stains, and fresh chew all over them. They were absolutely filthy. Yet it seemed they would fit, so I popped them in my mouth, then turned around and made faces at the team. All of a sudden there was a roar of laughter. The 35 or so players thought it was hilarious. When Coach Buck saw me wearing his dentures, he didn't know what to do, so we started slapping each other and putting each other in headlocks. This may have been the funniest thing I had ever done on campus, both of us going at it like wild dogs.

When we finished, his hair was all ruffled, and chew was running out of his mouth. By now many coaches had run down the hall to find out what the scuffle was all about. All they could see were players falling out of their seats on the floor laughing as Coach Buck tried to get his dentures out of my mouth. I politely gave them back to him as the coaches started laughing. When practice started, Coach Buck seemed to have appreciated the prank, as he patted me on the back of the helmet. It was back to business as usual.

Chapter 25

Boomer Sooner Disappointment

S pecial teams were a blast. I would do anything for the team, although I had a burning desire to play more at linebacker. The Oklahoma Sooners were visiting, coached by Barry Switzer. He had a powerhouse of a team as usual. I had never seen such a well-groomed, athletic bunch of players. The more he won, the better his recruiting went.

By the third quarter against Oklahoma, we were really getting beat. I had given out six extra tickets to friends who had flown in, and I would have done anything just to get in at linebacker for a play or two. Don't get me wrong – I was thankful for every opportunity. I just wanted to contribute more.

Around the fourth quarter, I was reminded of the hardest lesson of being a walk-on. They put in a linebacker, a freshman again, one who I knew I could outperform – the same thing that had happened when we played against UCLA. The scholarship athlete sometimes plays instead of the superior walk-on player. That was hard on me. I had made it this far, but would I ever go any farther?

After this Oklahoma disappointment, I came directly back to my room. I wouldn't give up. I had to keep fighting. Sure, I was hurting, but they hadn't heard the last of me. I got down on the ground as field goal kicker Tom Field kept the stopwatch. It was good to have Tom, the doctor to be, at my side, as he had a calm and godly disposition. For the next 30 minutes I did 33 pushups per minute. In the last minute I did 70 extra. It came out to more than 1,000 pushups. I broke my old high school record of 1,000 in an hour.

This was my way of channeling my anger and frustration. I had to persevere. I couldn't always be everybody's all-American – I had to hang in there and fight. Honestly, I thought about quitting, yet I knew the sun would still come up tomorrow. One day I would pay the Sooners back! I learned to use drawbacks as inspiration.

Chapter 26

It's the Cone Brothers

As the season wore on, practice could get a little monotonous. Now and then fights would break out among teammates. All of a sudden, I would hear loud cheering from anywhere on the practice field and know there was a fight. All players would have to see who was involved. The staff didn't encourage this behavior, but you couldn't always stop two athletes playing with such intensity from having it out.

One play during practice, I was opposite my brother (linebacker vs. guard). Whenever we had a chance to beat on each other we would, so as the play ended we both went after each other under the bottom of the pile. As players were all being pulled off, the fight raged on. Like a well-rehearsed play, we rolled and rolled, swinging and kicking, kicking and swinging. Many players came running from all ends of the field just to see the fight. My brother and I could hear the coaches as they came to break it up. "Who is it? Who's fighting? Who is it?" Finally as the grad assistants pulled us apart, you could hear them say, "It's the Cone brothers." The coaches were all laughing as they walked back to the huddle, and we both saw Coach Fairbanks with his head down laughing.

CHAPTER 27

A Night Under the Big Top

D uring the middle of the week, an entertainment crew came onto campus and erected a huge white tent just outside the stadium. It was close to our dorm, Bracket Hall, just across the field. It was set up as a hospitality gathering area for the alumni club for that week's football game. Coach Ron Hubbard was responsible for hiring security under the big top and sent a message for me since I was a walk-on. No scholarship athletes were invited, as they would actually be playing a game on Saturday. I guess I was expendable.

I agreed to $75 to spend the night Thursday and $75 to spend the night Friday. That was a lot of money, as most of us had little coin in those days. Imagine being paid to camp out in the middle of Colorado's campus.

I had to be there from 9 p.m. until 7 a.m. I had always liked camping out, and the first night went off without a hitch. I had my pillow and sleeping bag to keep me warm, and I made an easy $75. At least 15 or 20 of my friends dropped by to either pull some stupid prank on me or just to say hello. Some of our gal friends from the sororities stopped in with some food. I slept at least seven hours. Other than a few firecrackers, smoke bombs, and water balloons, the night went by without a hitch.

Now, the second night was a different story. I made a deal with Ray to give him 30 bucks to spend the night on Friday to provide extra security. You know, I was just trying to spread the wealth. Others heard of the fun, and before you knew it, nine guys were now spending the night, not wanting to miss a thing. Every 15 minutes or so, a different player could be seen walking across the campus with his blanket and his pillow, heading for the big top. Some of the starters slept on the ground the night before a Big Eight game. We all took a vow of silence not to tell any of the coaches.

By now the crowd had swelled to about 12 players, some spending the night, others just wanting to see what was happening. In came our pal Greg from Greenwich, Connecticut. He was a talented walk-on wide receiver whose high school quarterback had been Steve Young. He just stopped in to bother us, as he had been feeling left out. Greg was a close friend, but off the record he was a bit of an agitator. Next entered LaWayne, another walk-on running back from Washington State, who I nicknamed "Night Breeder" because he would leave the dorm late at night not to return until who knows when. LaWayne was a compact tailback, and very feisty. We were all just hanging out when suddenly out of nowhere Greg must have said something, and LaWayne punched Greg in the mouth, knocking out one of his front teeth. Poor Greg stood there in shock. With my flashlight in hand, we all looked for Greg's tooth on the ground. LaWayne grabbed his backpack and strolled away into the cool night air. Was that ever a big story the next day around campus.

Later on around midnight some businessmen stopped by to find out what was under the Big Top. They couldn't see us, but we could see them, so we started to bark like a bunch of dogs. We about died laughing watching grown men running for their lives. Around 1 a.m. I snuck out of the tent and started howling like a wolf. Everybody told me to quit jacking around.

CHAPTER 28

Lat Patrol

Lat Patrol was the most fun we ever had in Brackett Hall. As far as having a blast with fellow players and keeping the team together, this was it. On the second floor, the huge bathroom had six shower stalls. One stall was an open air shower with no curtain, which hadn't been used in years. The shower had a strong, one-inch bar across the top, perfect for chin-ups. From the time I arrived at Brackett Hall, I would do five sets of chin-ups every Tuesday and Thursday night. My brother Ray would always join in. In honor of the 70s hit series *Rat Patrol*, the series Lat Patrol was born in Brackett Hall (chin-ups really work the lats).

On Tuesday and Thursday nights, my brother and I would form up around 9 p.m. He would go to his room to get his ghetto blaster with his Billy Preston *Behold* cassette. We would blast the music and start clapping. I would go up and down the hall yelling "Lat Patrol, Lat Patrol," and out would come anywhere from 10-15 guys, clapping, dancing, and forming a line behind the chin-up bar. Nobody would wear a shirt, and many of the brothers had nylons over their hair. Each player would do a set then rotate to the back of the line after stopping in front of the mirror. We would all do five sets of behind-the-neck chin-ups. I would start each player at reps they could do for five sets. We all clapped, yelled, danced, and encouraged each player.

Everyone made great gains throughout the semester. I would do five sets of 15 reps. My record that semester was 100 chins in five sets. Lat Patrol was a big hit, especially in a bathroom full of mirrors, and many of the Lat Patrol members were now walking around campus with a little more swagger. Lat Patrol was just what the doctor ordered as a nice 20-minute study break. It's amazing what you can do when everybody's all fired up. Every single athlete was able to set a new personal record.

CHAPTER 29

Badminton Anyone?

───────※───────

I was finishing my homework in our big beautiful Norlin Library around 9 p.m. and just minding my own business when my friend Artie Nelson from Brooklyn yelled out, "Hey, Maaaaaaarty, let's play some badminton." He and I were in the same badminton class. Don't laugh – everyone in the PE department had to take several classes like badminton to become proficient in teaching. It was just what I needed, a nice peaceful game of badminton with no stress, just pure relaxation.

We played several games. We were tied, three games apiece, and Artie called for the final tiebreaker, a game to 15. I would have to work hard because Artie had played competitive high school tennis back in the Bed-Stuy district of Brooklyn. Everything was fine until Artie's girlfriend showed up. I could tell this girl was trouble from a mile away. Suddenly he started to pick up his game and play like a man possessed. We battled back and forth. There was no way I was going to let him win, especially in front of her.

Artie served for game point. He thought he had served an ace and began to celebrate until I informed him that he had stepped over the line during his serve. Artie went ballistic. Before I knew it, he was in my face, and we were rolling on the ground of the rec center, fighting like cats and dogs. I had to get Artie in a headlock, as he was actually foaming at the mouth. I restrained him for at least two minutes until he promised to calm down. That entire time his girlfriend was kicking me and swearing at me and calling me a bully. I finally let Artie up, and he was still furious. His girlfriend was still calling me everything in the book.

I asked her where she was from, anyway.

She screamed "Nebraska!"

I said, "That figures."

Honestly, I don't know how she got past security. (You have to understand that Nebraska was our most hated rival.)

There must have been 40 to 50 people witnessing the melee. The crowd couldn't believe a fight had broken out over a simple game of badminton. They seemed to like my Nebraska crack. Afterward, I would often wonder if there were more of her kind grazing around our campus.

CHAPTER 30

No Big Red

I felt that things were going pretty well my sophomore year as we were hanging there in the Big Eight standings. Then one day before practice Coach Gary Cabe informed me that I would not be making the traveling squad for that weekend's game against Nebraska.

Coach Cabe was a great man who cared a lot for me. He softly explained, "Marty it's all a numbers game. They need an extra wide receiver, not an extra linebacker." He also told me that six other coaches had argued on my behalf.

He should have never told me this news before practice. I was devastated. For years I had looked forward to making this trip, ever since my Air Force days. I could hardly concentrate during the early periods of practice (20 periods total). I just went through the motions. Eventually I took myself out of practice and sat on the bench across the field. The head trainer, Ted Layne, came over to check on me.

I told him, "Ted, just let me sit here for the next two periods and then I'm gonna go down and start a huge fight."

Ten minutes later when the meat squad started around the fourth period of practice, I couldn't get this news off of my mind. I had had my heart set on going to Lincoln. As the offense broke the huddle, the starting center came out, got down over the ball, and then said something derogatory to me as usual. I was already seeing "Red." It was on. I backed up five extra yards then ran off sides and hit him with all my force. We rolled, punched, then tore at each other some more. All the coaches tried to break us apart, as I was fighting with our starting center. They had to pry me off of him. After adrenaline kicks in, it's hard to cool off.

That would be my hardest fight ever, as this player was super tough and would be starting for the Buffalo Bills the very next season. The coaches separated us and told us to cool off. I was screaming at everyone and was told to leave the field. As I passed Coach Cabe, I noticed a surprised look on his face. The center and I made up after practice.

Once again as a walk-on, I wasn't guaranteed anything. I thought for sure I deserved to travel, but I wasn't part of the plan for that week. I just had to keep showing up and hoping for the best. It made for a long weekend when my team was gone, brother, roommates, and all. I listened to the game on the radio. Wouldn't you know it, Roger Craig and Tom Rathman ran all over Colorado that weekend, and there wasn't a thing I could do about it. The radio announcer could at least have said hello to Marty, left behind back in Boulder and feeling sorry for himself. I laid low for a couple days so other students wouldn't see me. The big bad football player spent the weekend hiding in the dorm.

CHAPTER 31

Big Mark from Compton

<hr/>

S ometime during the season after the Nebraska game, Big Mark came into our room on a Sunday afternoon. He was about 6'5" and weighed 250 pounds solid. Mark wasn't an avid weightlifter, yet his body was long and lean with almost no fat. He had no idea of his potential. He had gotten scraped up against Nebraska and came down to visit about six of us players hanging out in my room.

We welcomed Mark in, not exactly with open arms but because he would have come in anyway. He was the toughest, meanest, and naturally strongest player I had ever seen. Wherever he would walk, it was like the Red Sea parting. To tell the truth, I liked the idea of having Mark on my side – I wanted him with me, not against me.

There in my room, Mark took off his shirt and said, "Let me show you guys something. Look here." He pointed to a three-inch blade mark. Then he showed us a couple of bullet holes and more scars.

Mark explained to us that this is how his life was back home in Compton, California. He literally had holes and scars all over his body. He told us that two times he had been left to die and had once been pronounced dead. Over the summer he had been in more than 30 fights. During one of his high school games back in Compton, Mark had been down in a three-point stance when he noticed dirt flying up all around him. After hearing gunshots from the stands, the entire team had run for their lives and piled into the team bus.

One day in the dining hall, Mark was alone in line as another tall, gifted athlete stood next to him. The player who just walked in was the Northern California high school wrestling champion (34-1). He was 6'4" and 240 pounds. Words were exchanged, and before we knew it the two behemoths squared off against each other. This was the scariest thing I had ever seen right before my eyes. Wild and well-placed punches were thrown as Big Mark beat this legend about half to death with little effort and left him there on the ground unconscious. That scared many of us players, and after that we were nervous about going near Big Mark. All of us saw him later that night back in the dorm, and he told us that fighting was just a way of life for him.

One Friday night about a month later, many of us headed to the Memorial Center on campus to watch a movie. We huddled in line outside the building, waiting for friends to show up. Just then, the campus police were summoned to the theater, and three deputies ran inside with their billy clubs in the air. It looked like the police were after someone big time. To our surprise, all three deputies came running out for their lives being chased by Big Mark, who had one of their billy clubs in his hand.

Colorado has produced some of the baddest dudes I have ever seen, guys like Ryan Mullaney, 6'6" and 255 pounds (LA Rams) and Leon White 6'5" and 400 pounds (LA Rams and professional wrestling, "Vader" and "Bull Power"). I once saw Leon White bench press 500 pounds for 10 reps. Big Mark was in the top three of the toughest players ever to set foot in Colorado.

CHAPTER 32

Norman, Oklahoma

The traveling list was up in the locker room after Thursday's practice. I was headed for Norman, Oklahoma. I was stoked. I could hardly catch my breath, as I sprinted to make a long-distance call to my aunt and uncle living in Moore, Oklahoma.

We made our way east to face the Oklahoma Sooners. I thought about the dust bowls, the trail of tears, land acts, and Boomer Sooner. I have great respect for the history of this region, and to be in Oklahoma in person was awesome.

We arrived at the stadium around 4 p.m. on Friday afternoon. Most players were a little quiet as we walked around the stadium, perhaps thinking of the standouts who had played on this very field: Billy Sims, Jack Mildren, Joe Washington, the Selmon brothers, the Owens brothers, J.C. Watts, Steve

Sewell, Steve Williams, D. Cumby, D. Hunt, and so many more I can't mention them all. This was a big-time venue, harboring a nationally ranked team every year.

The next day during warm-ups, head coach Barry Switzer stood on the sidelines with his staff. There was excitement in the air. I felt like a speck – my brother and I couldn't believe the stadium's enormous size. Around 80,000 people filled the stands. In came the Oklahoma Sooners behind that wagon mascot with those miniature ponies. I had never seen such a sight. The stadium was filled with a sea of red. Coach Switzer had built himself a quality program again. Their offensive line was huge, running backs quick and strong. The linebackers were big and fast, the most athletic players I had ever seen. During special teams, I had to work extra hard to position myself, as all these players had more team speed than I had ever seen.

They beat us soundly, and we had a great deal of respect for them. Afterward, I got to see my kinfolk. All my relatives from Oklahoma were there to greet my brother and me. They were so proud of us. My Aunt Nan brought along many members of her Baptist church – hopefully they had prayed for us and not the Sooners! A family reunion at the Sooners' stadium – how cool is that? In the parking lot, I asked the tailgaters for some food. The Oklahoma fans were such kind people and were honored to fill me up.

On that trip, I got to see five great running backs close up and personal. The best running back ever was Oklahoma's Joe Washington, along with Billy Sims and Marcus Dupree. Roger Craig and Mike Rozier rounded out the top five in my opinion.

I was still thankful even though I was a walk-on. This university had given me round-trip plane fare, a beautiful hotel room, a bus ride, taping in the training room, a fresh uniform, the chance to play in an amazing football game, and my name on every program. Just to be part of this great fraternal brotherhood was an honor.

It was Halloween, and all the players were dying to get back to Boulder for the famous Boulder Mall Crawl. All the weirdoes would be out in their insane costumes. On the plane ride, I sat next to my roommate, placekicker Tom Field. My brother Ray, across the aisle, informed us that he had given his fiancé an ultimatum to either pick a wedding date or break it off. He was confident that things would go his way.

Back at home, Tom and I checked out the Halloween festivities on the Boulder mall. Only in Boulder, Colorado, could you see such a spectacle. After a couple of hours, we returned to the dorm. Up on the second floor, we saw a huge player walking down the hall with his head down. It was my brother Ray. His meeting with his fiancé hadn't fared so well. She had given him the boot. When we heard the news, we laughed at him so hard we fell on the floor. We weren't trying to be insensitive – it's just the way we all ribbed each other. To be fair, it was rather hard on him. He'd been with his girl for a long time, as she had been his high school sweetheart from Lakewood High School.

To be honest, I was happy because she seemed like a know-it-all and always got on my nerves. Ray could never manage to spend much time with me, as she occupied his every waking hour. She would always show up at our workouts and get in the way, then come over to our place and offer me her pearls of wisdom.

Little did Ray or I know that the following spring I would introduce him to my good friend Patricia, a beautiful Chi Omega and extremely smart pre-med student from Tulsa, Oklahoma. She would later become his wife and bring five little Cones into the world.

CHAPTER 33

Texas Shootout

After Christmas break, we all returned to Brackett Hall. A walk-on quarterback from the plains of Texas brought his high-powered pellet rifle to campus. I told Ray this didn't look good. Sure enough, a contest was about to take place. Pizza boxes were lined up on the walls of this wrangler's room, and the target shooting began. After only one night of freestyle shooting, they expanded the target zone. The next day, the participants opened their door and the door to the room across the hall. Now there was cross-hall shooting to raise the ante. The rest of us knew it was only a matter of time. By the next night, targets were set up all the way down at the end of the hall. Now there was a full-scale dorm shootout. The number of contestants grew. The rest of us on that second floor wanted no part and went into our rooms and locked our doors.

By the end of the week, what a surprise, all the bathroom windows were now open even though it was freezing outside. Those boys had the novel idea to shoot at various targets and animals out of the windows. When we heard they were planning to shoot at birds and squirrels, we launched an immediate protest. A day later as we finished class, we saw an assistant coach carrying the rifle away from the dorm. Campus police were all around. It turned out that an engineering student had been shot in the leg, and the fired pellet had drawn blood. The actual target was supposed to have been the briefcase the student was carrying.

The marksman would go on to play eight years in the NFL. Nonetheless, events like these gave football and athletics a bad name.

CHAPTER 34

Mirror, Mirror, on the Wall

❖

Tuesday and Thursday eight a.m. classes weren't very desirable. Students had to get up early, and classes were close to an hour and a half long. We were barely awake. My eight a.m. anatomy and physiology class was torturous, one of the most difficult 400-level classes on campus. I studied an average of 25 hours for each major test. Many Colorado athletes and international Olympians were in this class. This professor was a former military doctor at a MASH surgical unit. He had no sense of humor, which made the class even less fun.

The sun shone brightly into the classroom, as all the windows faced to the east. I would move my desk near the brightest window clear across the classroom away from most of the students. I wasn't naturally smart, so I had to pay close attention and take good notes. However, one morning I was a little bored perched there in my window seat. I leaned my left arm on the window ledge and suddenly noticed a reflection from my watch on the wall in front of me. That was pretty neat – I could actually control this little ball of light. The farther across the classroom I would angle my watch, the smaller and more precise the ball would become. I practiced for awhile and slowly moved the ball of light on the ceiling across the classroom above my brother and the rest of the class.

The professor was intense. You didn't dare interrupt his class. He was not only a former medic and doctor but also a top-notch professor. A thought came to mind – should I interrupt the class and shine up his bald head with my new reflector kit? While I certainly didn't want get in trouble with the athletic department, I nonetheless gave into temptation and shined the ball across the room up on top of his bald dome. Then I quickly turned it away. My brother and several other players in the class were writhing with laughter, their heads down on their desks. Did I put my new toy away and show some respect and maturity? Not just yet. I again shined the ball of light on his head and then slowly worked it down and lit up his mouth while he was speaking. By now, some students were laughing out loud. The professor got irritated, so I quickly put away my little ball of fun.

After class, a decathlete from Germany told me he needed this class to graduate and begged me to please stop goofing around. Still, he admitted that it was the funniest thing he and his girlfriend, Nanette, had ever seen. Nanette was Sweden's top female athlete and Olympian.

I apologized to all and knew I would have to find a new pastime. The good news is that the ball of light only appeared two more times that semester. I settled for a B in the class, but talk quickly spread around the campus of the free light show.

CHAPTER 35

Double Ham Man

———————◆———————

During my first couple of years at Colorado, I had the time of my life being part of the football program. I was a walk-on, and nobody owed me anything, so I was never going to take one day for granted. I would always volunteer whenever a coach needed an extra body on the field at any position, anytime, anywhere. Walk-ons would do whatever they could to get noticed – all except one certain player.

This guy was about 5'8" and 175 pounds with a solid muscular frame. He had long, thick black hair. I never knew his name, as he spent most of his time hanging out with his girlfriends near the stands. Whenever he got the chance, he would run over to hug and kiss these two gals on the sidelines. The three of them were like a sideshow attraction. I never saw him volunteer for anything. As a matter of fact, I never saw him even get to practice on time to stretch with the team. Most of the time he would just show up to practice whenever he felt like it. The only thing we ever saw him stretch was his lips when he was kissing his girls. For all I knew, he could have been a campus employee or a Boulder model. I wondered if maybe Nebraska had sent him here to infiltrate our team. Or maybe, as some suspected, one of our coaches knew his dad.

One day he got the call. Coach Fairbanks screamed for a wide receiver, and onto the field he ran, leaving his harem on the sidelines. I looked at my position coach Bart Roth. We both agreed this could be dangerous, as we had never once seen him stretch.

A streak pattern was called, which would be a dead sprint down the sideline. The ball was hiked as he sprinted as fast as he could down the field. Here was his chance to impress the entire staff, make a name for himself, and impress his babes. Suddenly a loud scream pierced the air as the mystery player fell straight down on the turf. The ball sailed on by, only to be followed by a second scream. He was really hurt. Many team-mates gathered around. Head trainer, Ted Layne, and all the other trainers were quick to his side. The diagnosis was swift. He had pulled both hamstrings on one play.

Coach Fairbanks wouldn't allow his girlfriends down on the turf. We were laughing out loud as his two girls hung over the rail crying for their fallen man. From that day on, he would be affectionately known as "Double Ham Man." If he had an extra hamstring he would have pulled all three. His girlfriends saw him as some sort of hero. I never got his name or his history, yet I would still say hi to him when I saw him limping around campus with his shirt always unbuttoned and no backpack.

CHAPTER 36

The Walk-on Walks Off

It was late in my sophomore season of Big Eight football, and I had a deep desire to be in the greater rotation with the starting linebackers. We had won only two games after eight weeks of football. I had put in two hard years of work on the scout team against the starting varsity offense. I had learned the ins and outs of my inside linebacker position. The season was quickly drawing to a close with only two more games to go. That's when I found out that the staff had just moved another freshman linebacker ahead of me. I was still learning the hard life of the walk-on. At practice the day before, our quarterback had taken a one-step drop and thrown a bullet pass right over the middle at a high rate of speed. I had put both hands in the air, trapped the ball in my hands, and then run back the interception right through the offense. Half of them hadn't even known that I had intercepted the ball. I just knew I could play on the varsity team. But what made sense to me didn't always make sense to the powers that be.

We were deep into Wednesday's practice when Coach Fairbanks made a comment on how weak our scout team was. He then kicked us all off the field. I took exception to his statement and stayed right there in my position. He told me to leave with the rest of the scout team. Again I refused. The other coaches remained silent, as they knew what was about to happen. I threw my helmet as hard as I could at all the offensive coaches. All the inside pads flew out of the helmet as it bounced across the field to the sidelines. I then threw my shoulder pads, gloves, and arm pads as far as I could in all directions. At the 50 yard line, I ripped my cleats off and threw one at the starting defense and the other at the trainers.

I had just about had enough. All I wanted to do was help the team to win. To ridicule us like that was more than I could take. I then proceeded to walk off the field, yelling at everyone who was looking at me or laughing. By that point, all I had on was my ankle tape and shorts. I wanted to fight all the team managers and trainers. I yelled out to the kickers and punters that I would fight them all. My tirade lasted three minutes at least.

A 20-minute shower was just what the doctor ordered. Still mad, I didn't regret my decision to quit. I then lifted weights right below the team locker room. As I finished my workout, the team made their way in, another practice on the books. A bunch of players told me that my walk-off was the funniest thing they had ever seen in their lives. Many tried to console me as they felt for me and my plight as a walk-on.

Late that night, a position coach stopped by my room and encouraged me to come back to the team. He told me not to take any comments personally, as the head coach never meant anything by them. He just had mega pressure to win. I understood that. The position coach told me to keep hanging in there and assured me that someday I would get my chance. He also told me that the coaches really appreciated me. That was all he needed to say. I assured him I would be back out there the next day.

At the next day's practice, I could hardly believe my eyes as all my equipment had been restored to my locker and was ready to go. All my pads and shoes were back where they belonged, and the managers had even put my helmet back together. It felt good to be back even though I had only been gone a short time.

I had never meant any disrespect. I only wanted to play. I just knew I could help if given the chance.

CHAPTER 37

A Leap of Faith

I t was a warm, beautiful day in April, and I was stuck in class. We had a guest speaker in our sports psychology class, and I was extremely bored. Dr. Dave Wardell was the professor and one of the most popular professors on campus. He was a handsome man with lots of nice hair and a mustache. He would work out during his lunch hour in Balch Fieldhouse, running, doing pushups, and chinning the bar. Dr. Dave was always encouraging his students, and he headed up the Fellowship of Christian Athletes.

I would always sit up in the classroom window, which had a nice wide ledge. To offset my spring fever, I would often gaze out to the street to watch students pass by.

There was a nice, tall tree about 10 feet away from my second-story perch. Nearly 25 feet separated me from the ground.

I would often contemplate if I had the ability or courage to leap off the ledge and land on the tree of freedom. That day, I couldn't stand another minute of this class, and this beautiful 77 degree afternoon was beckoning to me like the sirens of old. I desperately needed to escape.

The outstretched oak tree was calling out, "Bring me your tired, your poor, your bored!" I quietly put my backpack on, waved goodbye to my classmates, and made like a squirrel. I took the leap of faith out of the second-story window and landed on an outstretched branch. The branch swung up and down so much I thought it was going to break. I quickly scurried down the trunk. Once on the ground, I beckoned up to my fellow classmates to leap out and join me, but there were no takers. I never knew what Dr. Dave thought about my early departure, and I forgot to ask. He just peered out the window with several classmates around him as I went on my way.

CHAPTER 38

Mid-Semester Book Sale

O ne morning after finishing my early classes, I was minding my own business as usual when I noticed something suspicious that caught my eye. Four tough, lean-looking, football players were walking across campus, each carrying a huge stack of books. I saw one carrying 15 economics books, one carrying 15 calculus books, one carrying 15 sociology books, and the last carrying 15 history books. I asked them what was up but got no explanation. I thought to myself, I certainly hope they aren't trying to sell back books in the middle of the semester. Later on after practice we all got the news. Four student athletes had been arrested for trying to sell back books they'd stolen from the athletic department.

The fact that they got caught was no surprise. First of all, it looks suspicious when four buff football players walk together across campus, each with 15 identical books in their arms. Then they had tried to sell their books at the campus bookstore. Maybe they hadn't bothered looking inside the cover of each book, which was stamped "Athletic Department – Not for Sale." Perhaps they told the person at the counter that they had taken each class 15 times.

One thing was for sure – once the word came down that they had broken into the Athletic Bookstore and stolen books, they were off the team.

CHAPTER 39

Who Will Stop the Paint?

I never did like change all that much. One particular day, as practice began, I noticed a crew of painters gathering around our dearly beloved black and gold end zone. To our shock and dismay, the end zone was about to be painted powder blue to match our new powder blue uniforms. All of us players were in shock. Without so much as a vote, our tradition was on the way out. The COLORADO letters would remain gold, but the black background would be powder blue.

Everybody watched and wouldn't do a thing. Didn't they know that evil prevails when good men do nothing? I had to spring into action. I started by throwing four or five rolls of tape at the painters. They came in like mortars in a combat zone. Then I kicked several footballs all over the end zone. I wasn't done. I had to do more.

While we were still stretching, I ran down the sidelines to unplug their extension cord. Then I jogged down to the opposite end of the field, where I tied the cord in a gigantic knot, covered it in athletic tape, and then quickly rejoined my teammates. Now the painters were mad. All of them went down to the opposite end of the field to find their cord. I sprang into action. I ran up the field and grabbed both of their five-gallon buckets of paint and ran them to the opposite end of the field without being noticed. Or so I thought. During the fourth period, I saw the campus police walking towards me. The police asked for #45 front and center. I was taken to the middle of the field for questioning in front of all my teammates. I admitted to everything and then began blaming the police for allowing this travesty to happen. To my surprise, one of the police was a former CU alum and didn't like the change either. They actually showed me respect and sympathy but told me leave the painters alone.

CHAPTER 40

Arnold's Diet Part 2

Our dear friend Arnold from Phoenix, Arizona, stopped by late one evening with something heavy on his mind. My brother Ray and I had been the architects of his diet the year before, helping him lose close to 30 pounds. Now Arnold wanted to lose another 20 pounds before spring break.

I told Arnold to report to my room first thing in the morning, and we would start off with 200 sit-ups. I went down the hall and informed my brother of the plan. We both enthusiastically supported Arnold's goals, as we would be staying at Arnold's house in Arizona over spring break in a little over two months. Imagine helping Arnold lose 20 pounds then being able to raid his home closet! We had eight weeks to help him melt the pounds away. It was on!

We all did sit-ups with pleasure to start each day. We would then meet Arnold for lunch and carefully scrutinize what he would eat. In the evenings, I would meet him for a light jog, followed by pushups and more sit-ups. Our plan went like clockwork as he shed the pounds. It helped as Arnold was stubborn and had lots of self-motivation. His weight went from 180 pounds to 160 pounds just in time for spring break.

We made plans to meet up at his house on the following Tuesday. We could hardly wait.

CHAPTER 41

Legs Up on the Competition

O ff we went, heading due south on our way to Phoenix for spring break. A nice, scenic, 900-mile drive, plenty of sunshine, and daily exercise. Just what the doctor ordered! Arizona is a paradise and a true athletic haven. You can work out, ride, swim, and golf, watch baseball, or just relax by the pool. We had sold vitamins, basketball shoes, rings, and CU apparel to help fund the trip.

We set off down I-25 around 9 p.m. in my teammate Tom's Volkswagen Dasher. I was the lead driver and navigator. After four hours, we crossed into New Mexico. Around the city of Raton, someone asked if we shouldn't fill up with gas. With my cross-country driving and former military experience, I said there was no need, as we were getting excellent gas mileage with the wind at our backs. They put full trust in me, and off we sailed into the New Mexico night. Then out of nowhere we were hit by severe headwinds. In less than an hour we were out of gas.

Thank the Lord that our friend Bill from Albuquerque was only about an hour behind us. When Bill saw us on the side of the road, he pulled over. We tried to match the bumpers but to no avail, as the profile of his Camaro was too low to the ground. We had no towrope and didn't feel like pushing for the next 50 miles. Suddenly I had an idea.

We lifted up the hatchback of our station wagon, and I crawled in the back with my legs hanging out. Bill pulled his car forward until his bumper touched my feet. Then two more guys got on either side of me with their legs hanging over and also touching Bill's bumper. Bill started slowly at first, then pushed us for 50 miles at 50 miles per hour. It was a bit scary, as all of us could imagine our legs getting snapped off, especially since Bill's Camaro would often swerve from right to left. We made it into Albuquerque around 5 a.m. I didn't mind the workout, but usually I like to finish before sundown.

CHAPTER 42

Spring Cleaning in Paradise Valley

A s we arrived in Arizona, our slender friend Arnold was there to greet us. We would be staying in his family's gorgeous home for the next five days in the beautiful Phoenix suburb of Paradise Valley. They had a beautiful, oval-shaped swimming pool surrounded by palm trees and desert landscape. As the members of our party were taking a nice relaxing swim, Arnold called my brother and me inside. We were ushered into his bedroom, where he showed us his closet. This closet was as big as any bedroom I had ever seen. Three collegiate athletes and their pet dog could have lived inside. We couldn't believe the amount of clothing before our eyes. Any fashion designer would have been proud of his collection. The sad news was that few of Arnold's clothes would fit him now that he had dieted again,. My brother and I proceeded to fill two trash bags with clothing. We went carefully through each item of clothing, taking 45 minutes at least.

As we left the closet, we could hear Arnold's mom pull up into the garage. My brother and I expected praise and high honor for carefully crafting out Arnold's new health program. Instead, she took one look into his closet and burst into tears. Thousands of dollars of clothing had just changed hands during this hour of power. We figured that we would all have to spend the night at the local mission. Arnold reassured her that the clothes were old and didn't fit and that he would be glad to go shopping to refill his closet. Soon the tears dried up, and we were invited to stay and have dinner. Thanks to Arnold, we had brand-name clothing for the next three years.

CHAPTER 43

In the Clearing Stands a Boxer

T he dinner bell rang, and before us was perhaps the finest table setting I had ever seen. Arnold's mom was wonderful and took great care of us. She placed a large platter of thick-sliced roast beef piled high on the table, along with gravy and mashed potatoes. We ate until we couldn't shovel in another bite. We thanked her dearly, but our gracious host informed us that we weren't finished yet. To our surprise, she carried in a gigantic plate of spaghetti and meatballs. We had eaten so much roast beef that we were absolutely stuffed, but we didn't want to let her down since she had worked so hard to make two main courses. (It must have been her Italian heritage.) We had to think of something quick.

The spaghetti smelled wonderful, and the meatballs were as big as tennis balls. When she left the room, I summoned the dog from under the table. He was a beautiful boxer about three years old, of fine pedigree and full of spunk. Within seconds, we gave the starving canine six meatballs, much to his delight. All I could hear was gulp, gulp, gulp, gulp. Did this fine creature not realize that digestion begins in the mouth? Our host returned and marveled at our insatiable appetites, and we were excused from the table.

As evening settled in, the boxer was nowhere to be found. We were all a little worried, as he had last been seen hours ago leaving the kitchen almost sideways full of meatballs! I launched a search party later that evening. Around 10 p.m. we found the beast passed out under a palm tree on the far side of the pool. He looked like he had gorged himself to death. He was lying under a ground spotlight, so I dragged him a few feet away. I poked his bloated stomach with a yardstick to virtually no response. He wouldn't move but was still breathing under his own power. After further investigation, I found out that all parties at the table had smuggled the listless boxer several meatballs. A recount showed he had devoured 16 meatballs! We feared we might have killed him.

Sleep came uneasy that night as I visualized an autopsy revealing 16 barely digested meatballs in his stomach. Restless, I snuck out at 3 a.m. to see if he was still breathing. All I knew is that we had less than $200 between the five of us, and I wanted to avoid getting kicked out at all costs. Should I tell the host that her dog had jumped on the table and eaten all the meatballs, or should we say the whole tray had fallen on the floor?

I looked across the yard in the pitch black of night. Military training kicked in as I serpentined across the backyard. From a safe distance I could tell the dog was breathing yet still lying listless under the palm tree. I dabbed a cool, wet rag over his forehead. Should I call the local vet hospital, I wondered? I prayed, then went back to bed.

We all rose at 8 a.m. and had a group prayer that the dog would survive. I glanced out the blinds and didn't see the beast, yet I didn't want to go out on the back porch because Arnold's mom was sitting near the door having coffee. We piled in the car and took off for our morning run. It was a hard workout with several 40- and 20-yard dashes.

As we returned to Arnold's house, we wondered if his mom would have noticed the missing dog by now and if our suitcases would be out in the street. I thought about spraying him with a garden hose to see if I could get him to his feet. Back at his house, we crept up to the fence and peered over. After nearly a 16-hour standoff, we had finally caught a break. In the clearing stood the boxer.

The boxer wasn't himself for the next few days. He looked like he had swallowed a football. Our host never noticed his condition, nor did Arnold. The beast passed gas all afternoon as we relaxed and enjoyed the pool.

Other than the boxer incident, spring break was nearly perfect. The smell of citrus filled the air, and palm trees waved in the breeze. Beautiful Camelback Mountain rose up from the Phoenix landscape. Spring training was in full swing, and ASU was just a few miles away, along with waterparks and outdoor movie theatres. We loved you, Arizona.

CHAPTER 44

Enter Bill McCartney

———————•———————

oach Fairbanks was a great coach, and I was thankful to him. After he resigned, we were introduced to our new coach, Bill McCartney, 42 years old from the University of Michigan. He also brought in a brand-new coaching staff. I couldn't see how this man had been let go from the Wolverines. A few minutes into his opening speech we knew he would be every player's dream. There was excitement in the air. He immediately laid out his expectations. We sensed that he was a man of his word, a man of discipline, and a real man of God. He taught us how to be men and to show respect for others. He was someone you could trust – the kind of coach that every dad in America would want his son to play for. We knew things were about to change. Coach Fairbanks' staff hadn't always enforced disciplinary threats, and some players had gotten away with murder. Not anymore.

When we first met Coach Mac, we could see he had battle scars and a slightly crooked nose from his time at Missouri, where he had been a standout Big Eight linebacker. There was no fooling this man. He knew every aspect of the game, and he was an enforcer.

That summer, my brother and I wanted to get into the best shape of our lives for our new coach, as he would put our conditioning to the test. He was going to find out who the best-conditioned athletes were. For me, as a walk-on, it was like having the slate wiped clean, as he treated us all as equals. Early in the summer my brother and I began doing more distance road work, long sprints, 440s, and rope jumping, only to start over the next day. Coach Mac had such an impact on us that we did more than we could have imagined. He was a gifted man, as well as a positive, encouraging speaker. We could hardly sleep that summer, anticipating his first season with us. We had a problem in the hot summer trying to keep weight on. We ate lots of peanut butter and jelly sandwiches along with protein shakes just before bed. If somebody would come back with too much added body weight, we were usually very suspicious that steroids were in play.

Several nights that summer I ran an extra 10 laps around the block at my house in Wheat Ridge. Each lap measured out to be exactly 440 yards. There's just something about running in the cool night air. I would do each lap in just under a minute, take two minutes to rest, and repeat the process nine more times.

I built a chin-up bar in my backyard out of one-inch pipes and two couplers. I did chin-ups two extra nights of the week to prep for our upcoming conditioning test. When I was feeling my best, I would try do a set of 50. I was able to set a new personal pushup record, completing 320 reps in five minutes. I did more than 15,000 pushups that summer. Our favorite running regimen was the following: 880s, 440s, and 220s, finished off with 20x40 yards and 20x20 yards, then stretch and stretch. Some days my brother and I would just run for distance. It always varied, one day distance, one day sprints.

The closer we got to the season, the more sprints and the more power cleans. I was able to bench press 315 pounds for 15 reps and 430 pounds for 2 reps. Parallel squats were at 440 for a set of 10. Dead lifts were around 575 for 5 reps, and cleans were at 280 sets of 5.

That summer may have been the most motivating time of my life. Upon our return to camp, it was time for our first physical challenge in front of our new coach. We were excited to show him what we were made of. Coach Mac took me to a higher level than I ever thought I could achieve. He had the greatest impact on my life.

The Best Conditioned Athlete Award was up for grabs. It was the most coveted award of the year. It would test each player with a co-efficient according to his weight, giving everyone an equal chance. I reported back that fall healthy, fresh, and in the best shape of my life. I had a lot at stake. I had to win the trust and confidence of this new staff. The Best Conditioned Athlete contest was on, and I hoped to win a scholarship.

For two solid days, we were tested on body fat, a mile and a half run, 40-yard dashes, dips, chin-ups, bench press max, and bench press repetitions at our body weight. The competition was fierce. Every single player wanted to win this award. Summer training had been self-paced. Nobody was there to watch you or push you. The main secret was never missing a workout and doing extra reps at night whenever possible. Consistency helped me more than anything. In addition, athletes from all over the country were competing against you, and many of them had won at everything they had ever attempted from childhood on. All the returning athletes were going to fight with every ounce of their being.

On the third day, the results were in. At our evening team meeting, Coach Mac took the podium. First he announced individual winners. I won the dips, chin-ups, bench press, and body weight bench press. I was in the top four in the grueling mile and a half run.

Then he announced the team's Best Conditioned Athlete: "And the winner is Marty Cone." He gave me a huge trophy and a handshake.

It's every walk-on's dream to start the season with a handful of trophies. You can never, ever stop when you're a walk-on. It was great to see all the new freshman, transfers, and junior college transfers looking at me. I was stoked for the upcoming season. And I was so thankful. Winning had been my number one goal, but there had been no guarantees. I thanked Coach Mac and thanked God for all the hours of training and for the strength to go on.

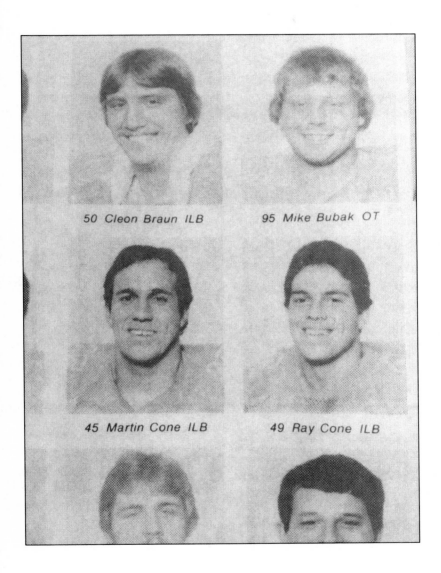

50 Cleon Braun ILB

95 Mike Bubak OT

45 Martin Cone ILB

49 Ray Cone ILB

One last time

ONE LAST PUSHUP—Marty Cone of Flight 0919, 3708th Basic Training Squadron (BTS) prepares to do his 249th pushup which broke the old school record of 167. Will Wady, physical conditioning instructor for the 3708th BTS squadron looks on. Cone is also a weight lifter having finished second in the 181 pound class in an all Colorado high school meet. (U.S. Air Force Photo by Sgt. George Prince)

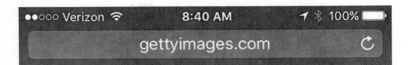

gettyimages   ≡

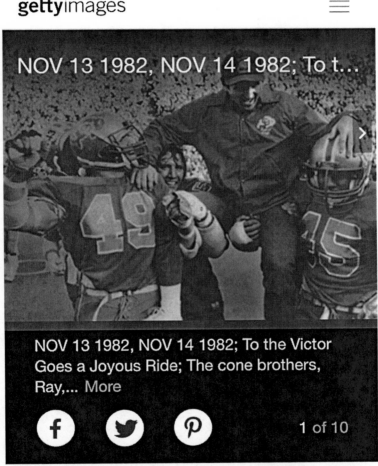

NOV 13 1982, NOV 14 1982; To the Victor Goes a Joyous Ride; The cone brothers, Ray,... More

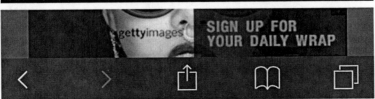

1 of 10

gettyimages   SIGN UP FOR YOUR DAILY WRAP

140

CHAPTER 45

Two-a-Days

Two-a-day practices were now in full swing. That meant two practices a day, all-day-long meetings, and films. Coach Mac was so well prepared that we started making great progress right away.

One night that summer, I decided to host a little competition. We owned an 185cc dirt bike, which we hid underneath the dorm in the crawlspace. My brother got it out that night. I had always wanted to see how fast I could ride the cycle through the dorm.

It was on. Tom held the stopwatch, and I maneuvered through all three floors in less than 90 seconds. My brother was second with 120 seconds. Others tried, but we were laughing so hard we could hardly stay on the bike, especially when our trusted friends were throwing oranges, toilet paper, wet towels, and leftover pizza boxes at us.

The next morning, just before our morning practice, word traveled around that a couple players had teepeed Coach Mac's house the night before. I suspected who had done it, but I wouldn't rat them out because we were a fraternity of brothers.

Coach Mac looked mad as he stood at the podium. The first words out of his mouth were: "Last night my home got teepeed, and Cone, I'm blaming you!" A hush came over the entire room, which was filled with all the players and coaches alike. You could have heard a pin drop.

I remembered from my military days to respectfully stand up for my rights. I stood and answered the coach: "That's impossible, Coach Mac. Last night I was competing in motor-cycle time trials through our dorm." Just then, the entire room broke out in laughter, even catching the coach by surprise. It seemed like that was the start of some fun I could have with our new staff, but I knew I would have to be careful.

That summer was extremely hot, but the two-a-days went by pretty fast. Halfway through the two-a-day practices, the Skywriters started to show up. This was a group of around 15 talented sports writers who would follow Coach Mac around everywhere he went. For the next few days, they would gather information about our team.

After one morning practice, it must have been 90 degrees already. A group of us players were walking up to the locker room from the lower practice fields. Knowing that Coach Mac was right behind us, I decided that maybe I should cool off a little. As we crossed the bridge over Boulder Creek, I jumped in the water in my complete uniform. I gathered a few large weeds and put them over my face, then yelled for help as Coach Mac and the Skywriters were walking by. Around 20 people stopped on the bridge and asked Coach Mac if the guy in the water was one of his players. He looked down at me, shook his head, replied, "No, I've never seen him before," and kept on walking.

CHAPTER 46

Tom Field and Friends

<hr/>

Tom Field was just what the doctor ordered. This 4.0 pre-med student would be my roommate for the next two years. The cheesehead from River Falls, Wisconsin, was our field gold kicker, as well as a two-handicap golfer and a standout high school wrestler and hockey player. Tom had two beautiful sisters, who would visit often, and a brother who was a fighter pilot in the Air Force. I remember him telling us his brother-in-law John Taft had tried out for the 1980 Olympic hockey team.

Tom was a good, churchgoing man, and he was into clean living, always flossing his teeth and oftentimes playing his guitar. I remember his stories of riding his 10-speed across 100 miles of the Wisconsin wilderness to his grandfather's cabin. He said he would pull off to the side of the road and spend the night in a forest under a tree. On one of his rides to the cabin, Tom was fast asleep under a bush when he felt one of his hairs being pulled out, only to awaken and see some old man walking away.

One day Tom invited me to one of CU's seven libraries. I had no idea where we were going. We entered the new building, and much to my surprise music was playing. This was called the music library. Soft classical music filled the air, making the room conducive to study. This became our favorite hangout. I learned great study habits from him. It's important to contemplate who your roommate will be. Choose wisely, as your decision will make a big difference in your college journey.

During the time Tom and I were in Boulder, I was the only one he allowed to cut his hair. I was his personal barber. While in the military I had spent many hours honing my haircutting skills. We would take a chair and an old sheet out on the sidewalk where everyone would be passing by. Tom would never say a word as his brown curly locks fell to the ground. Sometimes a crowd of 20 or 30 people stopped by and laughed. I told them, "There's no waiting in line at this barbershop." However, I never had any other takers. Before each summer, Tom would ask me to cut his hair super short, and then I would trim it up upon his return in the middle of August.

Artie Nelson, another good friend, was in many of my exercise physiology classes. He was a talented athlete who could run, bike, and swim competitively. He had been one of the best high school tennis players in Bed-Stuy in Brooklyn. He could play the guitar and was an outstanding photographer as well. (If you'll recall, he could also play badminton.)

One night as Tom and I were fast asleep, we heard a knock on our door. It was Artie on his last leg. His beautiful precious bride to be from Nebraska had just thrown him out on the street. We welcomed him in, heard his side of the story, then told him to put a sock in it and go to sleep. The next day, Artie was our new roommate. We were still in a small dorm, so he had to keep all his belongings under our desks and help keep the room clean or he would be out on his ear. It all worked out since we were best of friends. Tom and I both counseled Artie to never return to his ex, as well as warned him about dating any girl from Nebraska!

A couple of months earlier I had visited her and Artie in an adjacent dorm. I had noticed they had mice in her room that had babies. They were so proud to show me, but I thought it was absolutely gross. To top it off, they also had a Cocker Spaniel that had just had puppies. They were both so proud of the pedigree, yet the room stunk. Its like they had built their own ecosystem in that dorm room.

Our other part-time roommate was Zane from right there in Boulder. He would just drift in and out, as he wanted to hang around our room rather than go to his mom's house. Wherever he laid his backpack was his home, and many a night he slept on our floor. For the longest time he would only enter our room through our second-story window, always scaling the flagstone walls with pure athleticism. For the first two years, Zane always wore camouflage pants. Then one day I saw his legs and couldn't tell if they were really legs or if he was riding a chicken.

Everybody always fought to hang out around Zane. His sister Liz worked on the hill at Abo's Pizza. Whenever we were at the library, Zane would dash off to see Liz around 9:30 p.m. and bring us back an 18-inch pizza. He would have to smuggle it into the library under his army jacket, but he had no trouble going undetected since he was wearing full camouflage. We would put three cubicles together, say a quick blessing, and then eat the entire thing. Zane would always ride his motor-cycle up the stairs to our dorm and around our practice fields. He was always welcome, especially when he arrived with a pizza so big that he could hardly carry it.

We had many friends. Our friend Suzanne's dad owned a ski area in California. Another friend was Melanie, whose dad had starred in *Star Trek*. Yet another friend's dad was famous for musical scores in famous movies. Colorado University may be the greatest campus setting anywhere in the country for high achievers and their children – and for pure beauty.

CHAPTER 47

Football 101

———————————✦———————————

Not long after arriving in Boulder, Coach Mac quickly disbanded the football dorm. He felt that we needed to have our own private lives and not be with football players 24/7. So Tom and I now lived in a co-ed dorm. After a few short weeks, we had a good-sized group of friends. I quickly found out that many students weren't football fans, mostly because they didn't understand the game. Tom and I thought we should do something to help them.

We put up signs all over this gigantic dorm that read, "Football 101, Wednesday night, day room, third floor, 9 p.m." The response was overwhelming. About 40 students showed up, and the room was packed. We borrowed a projector and film from the football office. First on the agenda was to go over downs and distance. I drew up a position chart and named all the different positions, then I played some films showing real-life plays and examples. It worked out well. We then took several questions and answers. What a fun time! After the one-hour meeting, I handed out schedules and posters.

Don't assume that everyone knows your sport. It's real easy to take time to teach others, and the results will be fulfilling. We had just added nearly 40 new fans to the football program. The rest of the semester we were often stopped and asked questions about last week's game and what happens if this and that and so on. Some local hecklers even asked me how I got knocked down so easily in last week's game. Some weekends, students would even drop by with their parents to take a quick picture.

CHAPTER 48

Second Walk Off

—✦—

My junior year was the most fun I ever had, especially under this new regime. At times I was up to 230 pounds and working at nose guard, backup linebacker, and special teams. My first love and passion was still being on the scout team. It was where our new coach could get a firsthand look at any walk-on. Deep inside I knew I could be one of the top linebackers on this team, but I had to be content with my role of helping to make the varsity offense better. We struggled during Coach Mac's first year, but we could see his fire and determination to succeed. He wasn't about to give up. His staff were tireless workers. Assistant coaches would arrive at the football office at 6:30 a.m. and not go home until nearly 11 p.m. This grueling schedule wore on from August until February. I once heard it said that collegiate football coaches don't get a day off for seven months. Bless their hearts, they're doing it all for us. Most all of them have families.

As my junior year wore on, there came a time about 10 weeks in that I was growing so discouraged that I walked off the field, quitting for my second time. Yet another linebacker had passed me up the ranks to the varsity squad. I left Coach Mac a note letting him know I had enough. My 10-speed bike was in my dorm. Off I went on a 20-mile ride, as I was now training full time for the Ironman Triathlon. That night, the position coach sat down with me in my room. He asked what the bike was for.

I told him I had some training to do. He asked if it was because I had gotten passed over again at my position, and I told him yes. His response was something like, "tough luck – that's how it goes." That made me even madder. As a matter of fact, I didn't like this assistant coach at all. My roommate, Tom, and my brother Ray saw I was furious, and they were dying to know what the coach had said. When they heard, they started to laugh. We talked things over, and they were stunned that I really had quit.

As I prayed that night, I thought about many things. I felt consolation from God to keep fighting and persevere. I tried to take the focus off myself and think about the team. As a walk-on for three years now, I needed to stop feeling like a victim. I needed to keep up the hard work and remain thankful.

I would be lost without my football team. There was a greater lesson to be learned during my third year of playing for the Buffs. To live in Boulder was a privilege, and to be healthy and to be a part of this team were the best things that had ever happened to me.

This ability to be grateful would help me the rest of my life. If I could help anyone during a situation like this, I would say to remember that it's not always about you. Somehow you just have to swallow your pride. Start thanking God for as many things as you possibly can, and your problems will start to fade. (I also realized that I flat out did not like the position coach, which surprised me because I usually liked everyone.)

The next day, I showed up to the stadium when practice started. As the team was stretching, I ran the stands and did pushups down by the players so they could see me. Many of my friends were surprised I had returned. After running for 30 minutes, I had Ted Layne tape me up in the locker room. Then I headed back onto the field. As Coach Mac walked by, he winked at me, making it all worthwhile. I made a commitment to be as fierce a player as I could be. That was how I would pay him back. I made the travel squad that week again and was thankful. I thought a special angel was looking over me.

A player had quit in the middle of the season just a few weeks before. I remember seeing him on campus carrying his backpack, looking real smart and clean. He was a nice kid out of Arvada, Colorado. He told me, "You know, Marty, now that I've quit, more people are giving me respect than ever before." I wondered how could that be, since in my mind when you quit you're done. Nobody cares about some dude watching the game from the stands and telling everybody that he used to play. I'm glad I stayed.

CHAPTER **49**

Friday Night Lights Out

———————◦———————

I'm sure most everyone has heard of the football movie *Friday Night Lights*. As the season ends, the recruiting begins, and the coaches are off to land the best high school recruits in the country. West Texas has always been a hotbed for football recruits. Midland and Odessa High Schools often yield many Division I athletes.

Texas schools are known to have 30,000 fans show up for their Friday night games. Each year some of these Texas players were recruited to our campus. My brother and I were selected to be their hosts. We would escort these Texans in their cowboy boots, wrangler jeans, and letter jackets with 10 pounds of awards on their chests. They would often boast about how they would leave a big mark on this university. "I could be the big linebacker here as a freshman," they would say. Perhaps we should have opened our arms and welcomed them, but we didn't. Soon they would sign here at Colorado.

As the season began, we would meet them head on in drills. Don't ever underestimate a walk-on or any other player. You'll be up against players who have made football their lifelong dream. Picture some 18-year-old punk telling a group of other players that he's the real deal, ready to make his mark on us. The only mark we wanted to see was a target on his chest and back. During drills, we used our entire bodies as human projectiles. It's all about survival of the fittest.

And they would go flying to the turf with great regularity. I don't know if the coaches ever realized why we had so much added enthusiasm during these drills. If you're a recruit, it might help to keep your mouth shut! Don't come onto a campus boasting about how good you are. You'll get crushed in the weight room – and on the field.

CHAPTER 50

Low-Speed Chase Across Campus

I considered buying a Honda 70 mini bike, and I borrowed it from a fellow player for a month to try it out. I kept it in the trunk of my car. A couple of times a week I would ride it across campus or down to the stadium for a jog. One night I rode it to the library and parked it under a huge Evergreen. As I was leaving around 11 p.m., I saw Ray and offered him a ride back to Bracket Hall. That night, neither Ray nor I had any idea what surprise we were in for.

I took a secret path to cross campus under the protective shroud of nightfall. Ray enjoyed his peaceful ride in the cool night air, telling me I should buy the bike. As we passed the building with all the boilers inside, we saw two campus police cars directly ahead. It was too late – we had been seen. I don't know what came over me, but instead of dismounting and showing them my ID I drove directly between the police cars. It was on!

With sirens blaring and lights flashing, I was able to outmaneuver both police cars even though the mini-bike wasn't made for two larger people. (With our backpacks, we totaled almost 600 pounds.) "Dismount and put your hands in the air" blared from their loudspeaker. I disobeyed their direct order. I felt the need for speed and kept on even faster. My backup plan was to dump the bike and outrun the police on foot. I drove behind the dorms, back out to the fields, across a parking lot, and in between two more dorms. I then made a beeline for S parking lot, where we quickly dismounted and shoved the mini-bike into the trunk of my car. As we walked back to campus, several policemen rolled by us still in full attack mode. Boy, if they would have caught us it would have been curtains.

After a few more narrow escapes, I returned the mini-bike to its owner. Anyway, the handlebars were ready to fall off, and it would have cost too much to fix it.

CHAPTER 51

Where Did #45 Come From?

This game against Oklahoma State stood out for me even though I was limited to special teams. I remembered arriving in Stillwater, Oklahoma, to take on the Cowboys. It was a beautiful Saturday, and the stadium was packed. Homecoming was in the air. I knocked down a bunch of players before halftime. This was always a big deal, as each knock-down would make for good conversation on the sidelines. As I came running off the field, I heard constant threats from the opposing players.

I was on the punt team, standing next to my brother Ray. As the ball was kicked, I happened to see Okie State's punt return starting to form a wall to the left, so I yelled out, "wall left, wall left!" On the punt team, a player can't just run anywhere. Each player has to stay in his lane. As the return wall formed to the left, I snuck in behind the wall near the sidelines. The ball carrier came around the wall thinking he was home free. I popped out and leveled him right there in front of his sideline. His head coach ran on the field and said, "Where did #45 come from? One player stopped us from a touchdown!"

Later on in the third quarter, we punted again, and the same wall was set up to the left. I sprinted down, drifted left, and snuck in behind the wall again. Here came the ball carrier, gaining speed as he turned the corner, heading towards a perfect wall. Once again I popped out behind his wall and busted him out of bounds directly in front of his players and head coach. He screamed out, "It's him again! That same son of a bitch #45 stopped us from scoring again!" It's plays like these that I'll never forget.

At the end of the game, as I shook the coach's hand, he told me, "Nice job, son." I thanked him and said, "Nice game, coach." What a blast! Everyone has to do their part no matter how big or small.

During the game, our hands were full trying to contain Oklahoma State's running back, Thurmond Thomas, who would go on to be an NFL star for the next 13 years. With his slashing quickness, he was virtually impossible to stop. We also had a seriously hard time covering their powerful little punt returner who we could hardly catch, a guy named Barry Sanders who went on to become one of the most exciting running backs of all time for the Detroit Lions.

We talked about our individual conquests all the way back to Boulder. I felt like I was the most blessed player in the country after such a beautiful weekend. I was living out a player's dream.

CHAPTER 52

You Can Have Your Cake and Eat It Too!

———————❖———————

During a home game late in my junior season, the nationally ranked Nebraska Cornhuskers came to town. We were all coached up and ready to take the field. It would be a long afternoon for us, as the big red machine was in the hunt for the National Championship again. They had two Outland trophy winners on the line playing side by side. The running back would soon win the Heisman Trophy. Nebraska had a huge following, and even in our own stadium a sea of red flowed through the stands. Coach Mac would have none of that.

Just before we were to take the field, the defensive coordinator called all the defensive players into the shower room. He held a huge, flat box in his hand. He was crying well before the start of the game, which seemed a little fishy, and with a whimper he said, "Men, look what the University of Nebraska sent us!" With all of us huddled around, he opened the box. Inside was a huge, white sheet cake with large red letters saying, "We will rush for 1000 yards!" We could hardly believe our eyes. Several players quickly began to destroy the cake and throw it against the shower walls. Everyone was fired up. Some players had tears in their eyes!

I wasn't convinced. The Huskers had such a prolific offense that they didn't need to intimidate us with a cake. I wondered if it was an inside job masterminded by Coach Mac. I would have bet that the bottom of the box read "Boulder Bakery."

As the players began to assemble downstairs to take the field, I remained in the locker room. There was a beautiful, white sheet cake on the wall, some of it still intact. I dismantled a large chunk. It was nice and cold, the white icing fresh and thick. The texture was light and wonderful. I quickly downed it. I joined my fellow players downstairs. Once they saw me, some players were laughing so hard it's a wonder the coaches didn't send me home. Regardless, I was ready to play, and the cake hit the spot.

My brother Ray had cake on his face mask for the entire game. I later accused him of drinking the Kool-Aid, as he had fallen for the story and had tears in his eyes as the contents of the box were revealed.

CHAPTER 53

My Greatest Hit

E very linebacker has several great hits throughout his high school and college career. Every time I was able to knock a player to the ground, I felt the satisfaction of a great hit. My greatest hit would be against Oklahoma my junior year. It was a home game in Boulder, where we took on the mighty Sooners. At the start of the game, I had many friends hanging around the railing just behind us players. My friend Artie had several tee shirts made for my official fan club. What a pleasant distraction to see my gang hanging over the side rails with bananas and extra food for my brother and me. What a blast, as this game would be as much fun for them as it would be for me. There were even four students from Germany in my humble fan club, including Wolfgang Shoyseboigan and Ulrich Kiick. My fan club had no international barriers. I was honored.

We had just scored. The ball was kicked into the end zone, but a penalty flag was thrown on Oklahoma's 20 yard line. A personal foul was called against the Sooners, so we would re-kick from OU's 45 yard line. Our kicker had planned to kick the ball into the stands. I stopped the game, called the entire kickoff team back together, and told our kicker, Larry, to kick a "pooch" kick very high and make it land on or near the goal line. With good coverage, we should be able to pin OU back near the five yard line. Larry was very talented (Green Mountain High School, Lakewood, Colorado), and I told the kickoff team that Larry would kick it so high that we should be able to take a free running shot at anyone standing near the goal line. I knew exactly what was about to happen, as I had watched Larry practice this exact kick many times before. Players from the opposing team would be looking straight up as the ball was on its way down.

It was ON! Larry's kick was absolutely perfect, and it slowly drifted down towards the goal line, I had just sprinted 40 yards, when sure enough I noticed a blocker on the five yard line looking up at the ball. By the time he saw me, it was too late. My plan worked. I hit him so hard at the five yard line that we both landed in the end zone. My collision sent him 15 feet though the air, landing him 2 feet beyond the goal line. The entire south stands were cheering as they saw the hit! I actually shocked some of our players who saw the hit. I left the poor dude lying on the ground as his fellow players tried to put his pieces back together. Remember this is football, hit or be hit! I was so jacked-up I couldn't wait to take the field again. We were beaten by Oklahoma that day, but we could see that Coach Mac was closing the gap little by little.

The kicking game went well except for one particular play. Coach Mac had told our punter earlier in the week not to punt the ball anywhere near Marcus Dupree. He was another one of OU's great recruits, perhaps the most highly recruited athlete in the nation. He was 6'3" and close to 235 pounds and could have been on the U.S. Olympic team in the 100-yard dash. Our coach had told us to kick the ball out of bounds, kick it sideways, or kick it short – just don't kick it to Marcus.

My brother and I were out for the first punt of the game, and to our surprise our punter kicked the ball directly to Marcus. Marcus fielded the ball on a dead run and was off to the races. My brother and I couldn't so much as lay a hand on him as he blew right past us, which had never happened before. We looked back only to watch him dance across the end zone. Coach Mac had his head down in disbelief on the sidelines, and it was embarrassing running off the field.

We had never seen any player that size with such great speed. I didn't even have a chance to yell at him he was so fast. I think he had four touchdowns that game. He was like an NFL star playing against a bunch of rookies. Talk about unlimited potential.

CHAPTER 54

Wait a Minute, Coach Mac

———————✦———————

Another beautiful, sun-shiny day in Boulder, Colorado. The Kansas State Wildcats were all huddled up awaiting the running of Ralphie the Buffalo with the 80 Colorado Buffs in tow, ready for battle. This would be a special day for me as again several of my closest relatives would be in the stands. I had been able to commandeer many extra tickets from younger players for my family. Coach Mac gave us a final pep talk. He needed to win this game badly.

As the opening kick sailed down the field, I was in a dead sprint. I had studied the ball carrier on film and knew that he would run straight ahead then cut outside. As he made his cut, I was waiting for him and made the first tackle of the game. I was so excited to be able to perform in front of all my relatives and have my name called over the loudspeaker. I waved to all 10 of them just 25 rows high. Out of nowhere Coach Mac came running onto the field and got in my face, yelling, "Cone, you don't know anybody up there, understand." He wanted our undivided attention. I didn't like him yelling at me for simply acknowledging my family. They deserved some of my attention as well.

Early in the second half we scored again, and I was down in my stance on the kickoff team. Oh how I wanted to make the tackle again and again. Sprinting down the field as fast as I could, I smashed into the front wall of blockers then bounced off directly into the oncoming ball carrier to make another solo tackle. As I heard my name over the loudspeaker, I was beside myself once again and gave several fist pumps to my relatives and friends up in the stands. They were all on their feet cheering for me. This time, Coach Mac ran all the way out to the hash mark to yell at me once again. At a much higher pitch, I heard, "Cone, you don't know anyone up there." That was all I could take, so I grabbed my head coach by the shoulders, spun him around, and pointed up to the stands and said, "Wait a minute Coach Mac! From left to right, that's my brother Tom, my mom and dad, and my two uncles and cousins."

He yanked himself free and went back to the sideline where he belonged. I hadn't meant any disrespect. My excitement was hard to contain. On the sideline, several players were astonished that I would put my hands on our head coach. I told them I had wanted Coach Mac to meet my family.

Monday at the dining hall, Coach Mac apologized, telling me he shouldn't have run out on the field. We both just laughed. What a great coach and friend. He just wanted to win.

CHAPTER 55

Poor Artie

Our dear friend Artie may have been our biggest supporter. Being such a gifted athlete, he would have given anything to be part of our team. He was close to 6'3" and weighed 155 pounds, a talented string bean of a guy. Out of the blue I came up with an idea.

Tom and I found Artie after practice and told him the team was having tryouts for punter this coming Thursday. Tom gave him a ball to practice with for the next six days. Artie was beside himself. Artie carried that ball with him everywhere, to class, to dinner, and off to practice whenever he had the chance. Early in the morning, just outside the dorm window I could hear Artie practicing for his once-in-a-lifetime chance.

Three days before Artie's tryout, we all walked into class. Naturally Artie was carrying his personal football with him.

We sat next to each other in the back of the room. My brother was sitting up in front on the right side of the classroom. While taking notes, I noticed my brother motioning to Artie to toss him the pigskin. Artie looked like he was thinking about tossing the ball to Ray, so I asked him, "Are you out of your mind?" I knew my brother either wouldn't catch the ball or would throw it back to Artie at some high rate of speed. Neither scenario was a good one.

A few minutes later, Artie threw the ball to Ray as the professor was writing notes on the chalkboard. I looked at Artie with total surprise because I knew the missile was about to be launched back. I got up and moved my chair five feet from Artie. Sure enough, my brother waited a few minutes, then when the professor wasn't looking he stood up and threw the ball at Artie as hard as he could. It bounced off Artie's hands and hit the back wall. The professor was furious and demanded to know what was going on. Artie said, "I'm sorry, I dropped the ball." I thought it would be curtains for us all. Luckily the professor had a sense of humor. Word spread quickly around the team about that day's class. Everyone knew that you should never put Ray to the test.

On Thursday, three days after the classroom incident, it was time for Artie's moment of truth. Would he be Colorado's new punter after the 3 p.m. tryout? He was certainly poised and ready, looking strong at midfield, ice in his veins. He was all decked out in his Colorado tee shirt and his Frank Shorter running shorts that only covered about eight square inches of his loins. With 12 balls next to him, I encouraged him to kick as many as he could. That way, the coaches could see as many of his punts as possible as they entered the field.

By now the entire team had begun stretching with Artie only a few feet away. Artie gave his best effort and got in at least 10 punts. The coaches came up to Artie and asked him what he thought he was doing. Artie answered with an unusual confidence that he was here for punter tryouts. Coach Tanner asked him where on earth he had heard that we were having punter tryouts. In front of the entire team and staff, I could hear Artie say, "Marty Cone told me." I think the team laughed for five full minutes as poor Artie saw his plans dashed before his eyes and was escorted off the field.

Later that night we comforted Artie with pizza from Abo's on the hill.

CHAPTER 56

The Day Big Tony Came to Town

Just after our junior season, recruiting was in full swing. Many of the coaches were back from their trips, and recruits were starting to show up on campus. I was summoned to the coach's office and given an important assignment. Big Tony had arrived on campus, and I was selected to take him out for a night on the town to familiarize him with Boulder. Many coaches informed me of just how important it would be to land this top national recruit. Tony was 6'5" and weighed 260 pounds. Every team in the country wanted Tony on their team this coming fall. We were honored to have him visit our school.

I had every intention of making Tony feel welcome and like one of the guys. As I arrived at the coach's office, I was treated like something special. It was an honor to be selected to host this top recruit. In the reception room, I recognized Tony instantly. There stood one of the most awesome athletes I had ever seen. It was easy to see why every nationally ranked team in America was after him. He was as big a player as I had ever seen, yet he was only 18, a handsome, buff, Hispanic-looking dude. He could have been on the cover of *GQ*. Maybe I had been selected to host him since I'm half Spanish (my mom's maiden name is Baca). I introduced myself to him, and we hit it off like brothers. We left for a fun-filled night on the town. Neither of us had any idea of what was in store for us.

Several of my friends wanted to go with us, as they had heard of the legend of Big Tony. Next thing I knew I was driving through Boulder with nine players in my car. We started off with a gigantic steak dinner at the Broker Restaurant. Naturally, most of the players who weren't invited had no money. I had to use my credit card, which had only a $300 limit, to help settle the bill. (My friends assured me they were good for the debt.) Soon we were off to the Fiji fraternity house for their annual beach party. As were arrived, we could hear The Beach Boys' music playing in the distance. I cautioned Tony and all my fellow players to be on guard, as some of these little frat rats will drink beyond their limit and jump out of the crowd to take on a football player. It makes for a big story the next day to say that they had mixed it up with a big, bad player.

We were welcomed inside the party, and Tony seemed to be having a good time. But we weren't there 20 minutes before some dinky, fueled-up frat rat jumped in Tony's face, swinging for no reason. Tony sent the poor little dude sailing across the room. I quickly joined in – as if he needed any help. By now several of us had formed a natural perimeter, launching frat boys into the pantry and off the walls. Finally no one else came at us, and we left a trail of bodies strewn all over the room. On the way out, I told the frat president just how stupid his frat was. I said that was no way to treat such a prize recruit or anyone for that matter. We laughed all the way to the car and then some. It was actually one of the most enjoyable times we ever had.

Next we headed to the Sigma Nu "rock and roll blowout" party to show off Big Tony. We were welcomed with open arms, as I knew some of the brothers and pledges. They all were pretty impressed with Big Tony's size, and many people encouraged him to sign with CU. Tony was handsome, and my stock soared through the roof. I thought maybe some of those girls would ask Tony, "Who's your friend?"

We stayed about an hour and had a pretty good time. As we were leaving, another peewee frat rat told us we were a bunch of losers. We just laughed at him. He wore his collar up on his Izod shirt, which we all thought was pretty stupid. It was funny until he jumped onto us and started swinging. Now eight of us were fighting on the front lawn as the frat house quickly emptied. At least 20 people joined in. All I remember is a bunch of screaming and people flying through the air. To add fuel to the fire and make Tony laugh, I pulled the frat rat's shirt over his head and started spanking him with his topsiders. Once our perimeter was set up, we encouraged more opponents to take us on. As we drove off, Tony was ecstatic, having had the time of his life. He held his stomach from all his laughter.

We were now headed down Broadway with nine players in my car and one on the hood. Even though we were having fun, I had to be careful not to let the player on my windshield get hurt. I don't know what compelled me to throw my bottle of Gatorade on the hood and spray him with wiper fluid. We were all laughing so hard that I could barely drive. We all wondered what we would tell the cops if they pulled me over. I said I would tell the cops that the player on the hood had fallen out of a tree and landed on my car. That got Tony laughing hard.

By then it was getting late, and we had to get Tony back to the hotel to meet with the coaches. As we pulled into the parking lot, a fully lit cigarette came flying in my car, bouncing off Tony's chin and onto my floorboard. A hippie-looking dude was sitting on the curb, and I asked him why he had flicked the cigarette into my car.

Before I knew it, his girlfriend had jumped on my back and clawed me as hard as she could while her boyfriend went for my legs. Many players pried her off of me, as my forehead and face were bleeding. I subdued the boyfriend, which took little effort. By now the coaches had all come running outside. An eyewitness told the coaches what had happened. Once again Tony was laughing so hard that his stomach was sore.

The next day at lunch, all the coaches asked me exactly what we had done the night before, as Tony had laughed all the way to the airport. Tony was gracious, and before he left he thanked all the coaches. Unfortunately for us he chose the University of Oklahoma over CU. For the next couple of years when we would play the Sooners, we would always give Tony a big hug before the game. Anytime he would glance over, I could still see him laughing. Four years later, Tony Casillas would sign with the Dallas Cowboys and become an NFL star.

CHAPTER 57

Four Miles for Nothing

O ne cold winter's morning as I was jogging in the field house, a popular girl on campus waved me over. Her brother was a collegiate tennis star here at CU. She was in tears, so I stopped my run to see if I could help. She asked if I would relay an important message to Coach Mac about her and a football player. She thought she was pregnant. I told her I would tell him around 4 p.m. when he would start his daily jog around campus.

Sure enough, at 4 p.m. there he was, stretching in the coach's parking lot. I figured I would take only two minutes out of his busy schedule. As I began to speak, he said, "Marty I can't talk right now, but please come along, and I'll hear what you have to say."

179

I had jogged with him on several occasions before, but I didn't want to jog with him this day as I had already run in the morning and had an intramural basketball game that evening. Still, it was the only way I could talk to him. As we started to jog, Coach Mac took out a piece of paper. Unbelievably, that paper contained the names of more than 500 people he prayed for every day. We ran for nearly 40 minutes as he prayed for each person on that list. By the time he finished, I was so worn out I could hardly talk. I couldn't believe how much discipline and heart it took to pray for 500 people every day.

When we made it back to the parking lot, he asked what was on my mind. Before I could get five words out, he said, "I already know!" Then he left, saying, "I love you, brother." I had just run four miles for nothing! I scored only eight points at my basketball game that night and had to sit out most of the fourth quarter due to exhaustion. Still, Coach Mac was really something. He always seemed to know exactly what was going on.

I saw the girl the next day and I was able to encourage her to protect life at all cost. No matter what, a child is a true miracle from God. The pregnancy turned out to be a false alarm. Thank God everything worked out.

CHAPTER 58

Run for My Life

O ne night in the dead of winter as we were driving the back roads of Boulder, my roommate's car was pelted with snowballs. I told Tom to pull over, and we circled back around on foot and caught the punks in the act. As we drew closer, we recognized every one of these lawbreakers: fellow teammates having some good clean fun. Naturally we joined in. (The coaching staff wouldn't have sanctioned such an act. It was a simple matter of trying to better ourselves with some hand-eye coordination drills.) We hit several cars and had the time of our lives. Then we hit a powerful, four-wheel-drive truck.

The truck sped around the corner, looking to run us down. From past outings, this was nothing new, so I had a planned escape route. We all took off down the alley like bats out of Hades. This time it was serious, as the enraged driver was bashing everything in sight. Trashcans were flying, and fences were being mowed down. All six of us were in a dead sprint, running for our lives, looking for cover wherever possible, hiding behind trashcans, telephone poles, garages, and vehicles. I saw a car and dove behind it for cover. I felt like a wise alley cat. After a few short minutes, I got up from behind the car, hoping that the coast was clear. As I backed away, I couldn't believe my eyes. Something about this car was familiar. I quickly called out to Tom. My heart was pounding.

It was my car. It had been missing for about three weeks. I hadn't called the police because I thought it would return someday. Sometimes players will borrow your car, and then their roommates think they can also borrow it without asking. In this case, I became the crime scene investigator, and, sure enough, it was out of gas. Somebody had probably used it to visit a babe, had run out of steam, and had abandoned it. We bought gas, started it up, and drove back to campus with a new lease on life. We all met up back in the dorm, still amped up after our near-death experience.

CHAPTER 59

To Do List

———————————————

It was early February of my junior year, and I would have a busy day today. So busy that I had made a list: do laundry early, re-copy notes, return books, see professor at office hours, quit football, fix sunglasses, and workout. I had walked by the coach's office a few mornings before. The blinds had been open, and I had been able to see the depth chart from the parking lot window.

After all the years I had put in, I was still low down on the depth chart at linebacker and nose guard. That was it. I had had just about all I could take, so I wrote Coach Mac another letter. I had just quit back in November, but this time I would call it quits for good. I snuck into Coach Mac's office and strategically duct taped the letter to his desk next to his mountain of mail.

183

He would see my letter first, as it was next to his Bible. I had my own "proverb" ready for him.

That evening, Coach Mac stopped my brother and my roommate, Tom, in the dining hall and told them that I had quit again. For the next two to three days, I went into hiding, keeping a low profile. I wouldn't allow anyone to talk me back into playing. At 24 years of age, I wasn't a baby trying to get my way. I was just tired of empty promises and still no scholarship. During the off season, it's easy to quit because you really don't miss anything. Now I was training full time for triathlons. I had learned how to swim in advanced lifesaving class and had gotten certified to be a lifeguard. I had a decent bike and could always run. Free at last, free at last, praise the Lord I was free at last.

A few days later, one of the defensive coaches, Dan Coen, found me while I was working out in the field house, running laps with Frank Shorter. Maybe I should qualify that statement; I was on the same track with Frank Shorter. (Remember, he was the gold and silver Olympic medalist in the marathon.)

The coach said, "Cone, you're making a big mistake. Have you seen the new depth chart?"

I told Coach Coen that I had seen it a few days earlier and that I was no longer part of the team. He asked me to please check it out one more time.

We always had a fondness in our heart for Coach Coen. He looked like a mountain man and drove a Harley everywhere he went, even in the winter. On road trips, oftentimes he would wear biker boots. We even invited him over for movie nights throughout the semester. I made him watch *The Man from Snowy River* several times with us. He always looked out for us.

After a great run next to my Olympian friend, I snuck over to the football office, where I could see the revised depth chart through the window. I was shocked to see I was now the starting inside linebacker. Suddenly I was revitalized again with a new spirit. This time (my third time quitting) I had been away only three and a half days. It was just one of those down times I had had to work through. I felt better now that I was back with my football family, no longer having to be in the wind hiding from the team.

CHAPTER 60

Spring Fitness Tests

───────────❖───────────

C oach Mac put us through some grueling tests early that spring. He brought in Brad Bates to be our strength coach. Brad was a former standout player of his from the University of Michigan, a physical fitness phenomenon in his own right. He was Michigan's best-conditioned athlete, sporting less than four percent body fat. For the next six weeks, Coach Brad would just about kill us. As the newest official member of the team, I was ready. I had to make these tests count. It would be my last spring, as I would be a senior in the fall.

The first test was the parallel squat with our body weight. Coach Brad said that the standing record was 50 (parallel) reps. I always waited until the end of the testing day before I would compete. That way I knew who had done the most reps and who I had to beat. With 225 pounds on the bar, I cinched up my weight lifting belt, tightened up my super wraps around my knees, and began to squat. I did the first 20 reps parallel without stopping. (The only way to do a legal, correct squat is to break parallel.) I then did reps, 40, 50, 60. I had to stop at 65, my new record and our new team record. I had done 65 reps at 225 pounds without stopping. By now I could hardly stand upright. Later on Coach Brad admitted that the previous record of 50 reps had been bogus – he had made it up! My brother Ray had done the most with 30 reps. Coach Brad had inflated the results to get the most out of me. The next day, my roommate, Tom, had to carry my books to class because I walked like a primate. With my lower back and legs in pain, I couldn't stand erect. I would have to miss lifting for the next two days.

Three days later we had the dead lift test, pulling the bar off the ground and standing straight up. The record had been set by Ray and Jeff Donaldson (Atlanta Falcons), each doing 22 reps. With 225 pounds loaded on the bar, I finished two hard sets of power cleans, as this is the best way to warm up for dead lifts. Dead lifts are hard, and I needed to be psyched up. I got to 20 reps fairly easy, then 30, then 40, finally stopping at 44. Another new record! My back was so worn out I could barely stand up straight. Now for the second time in less than a week, Tom carried my books to class. I couldn't work out for the next two days.

The bench press test was next. I loved this type of competition, especially coming from my powerlifting background. We first did the max-out test. I lifted 440 pounds and barely missed 460 pounds. My 440 effort tied me for the Big Eight record with Thomas Benson from Oklahoma. The next week, I managed 450 pounds, which set the Big Eight linebacker record. However, Coach Brad wasn't done yet. We next tested our body weight bench press. I loaded 225 pounds on the bar, tightened up my four-inch wide belt, and began to do reps. I did the first 25 reps without stopping, then continued on to 30, 35, and 40, stopping at 44 reps. I set yet another new record, doubling my closest competition. I always knew that doing all those pushups and parallel dips was the key to bench press repetitions. (Remember, don't do pushups the night before you bench press.)

The following week, I took first place in the University of Colorado's bench press contest. Two weeks later, I won the Colorado State Bench Press title in South Denver. In the room were a bunch of big studs whom I had competed against in high school and many other meets. When you show up for the competition, everybody tries to size you up. To blow them away is indescribable. Thank you, Lord.

CHAPTER 61

Down and Out in Mesa

———————✦———————

My roommate, Tom, and I had an idea. This year we wanted to fly to Phoenix for spring break. To earn money, we passed a flyer around to local neighborhoods saying we would rake leaves, pull weeds, paint, and even remove animal droppings. Finally we landed a nice paint job, interior and exterior. During our easier school days, we would meet up and paint. It was spring, and the weather was beautiful in Boulder. The job took us almost two weeks part-time. We now had over $800, which made the trip possible.

As we arrived at Stapleton International Airport in Denver, we limited ourselves to only one backpack and a 10-speed bike each. We had to put our bikes in a box under the plane. I recognized the attendant working the gate from high school. As the 737 lifted into the air, Tom and I were comfortably seated in first class thanks to my lifelong high school buddy.

When you land in Phoenix, you deplane off on the runway. Men working on the ramp gave us our bikes. After adjusting the pedals and handlebars, we were now on our way. It was around 10 p.m., and we started our 25-mile ride to get to Tom's grandparents' house in Mesa. I would recommend this mode of travel to anyone, as our ride was peaceful, and we traveled in the cool Arizona night air. We arrived around midnight and stayed in Mesa for three nights. Then we loaded up our backpacks and were off again. This time we rode for 30 miles to North Scottsdale to stay with "Beak," Tom's hometown pal from Wisconsin who eventually got a job with the Phoenix fire department. Beak graciously let us stay for the week.

Tom and I were always competing against each other in tennis, running, wrestling, biking, etc. Everybody thought Tom was such an angel. I knew better. We weren't even 10 minutes into our 30-mile ride when Tom came up behind me and stuck his thumbnail deep into my back, which really hurt! It was on! He rode off as fast as he could. Furious, I caught up to him. Unfortunately our tires hit each other.

Naturally, Tom was unscathed; however, I went flying out onto the pavement in the middle of traffic, creating an instant traffic jam. I landed on my butt and was knocked out cold. Several people pulled over to help and dragged me off the pavement into a gas station parking lot. The paramedics eventually arrived. I finally came to but had to sit for several minutes until my head cleared.

An hour later, I was able to remount, and we continued our ride. One of the paramedics told me that since I had landed on my buttocks, most of the blood in my brain had gone to my posterior, causing me to black out. Many of my friends wondered how much I had in my brain to begin with.

I returned to Boulder with a huge purple bruise the size of a grapefruit on my right buttocks, only to receive scorn and laughter from the entire football team. That stinking Tom! I made him cut his nails and treat me to McDonald's!

CHAPTER 62

Down and Out in Farrand Hall

The football food training table was in Farrand Hall. We met there three times per day, and the food was great. One day after several of us finished dinner, we took a shortcut to our dorm through the halls.

It was around 6 p.m., and many room doors were open since most students were studying or just hanging out. We came upon an open door where many girls were studying. I sent them Tom Field. I shoved him into the room, and the girls all screamed. The rest of us left the dorm laughing our heads off.

A few minutes later, we all realized that Tom hadn't yet come out of the dorm room, so we went back to look for him. There he was on the ground of the girls' room, several girls administering to him. It turns out that when I pushed him into the room he had stumbled and hit his head on the bottom of a desk, which had knocked him out cold. Now Tom needed medical attention just as I had on our bike ride to North Scottsdale. We all felt bad but later laughed all the way back to the dorm.

That evening, Tom took it easy. He flossed his teeth around 9:15 and turned in early. I watched him sleep. He had a small shaved area on his head and a butterfly bandage. We were just a little nervous.

CHAPTER 63

Welcome, Coach Lou Tepper

E nter Lou Tepper, our new defensive coordinator and linebacker coach. He was brought in from Virginia Tech, where he had installed one of the top defenses in the country. He would put in his new eagle and hawk defensive package. Suddenly I found myself as the starting inside linebacker. I was no longer on the scout team; I would have to change my reckless style and become a technician at my position.

Coach Tepper is a great man, as well as a good, clean, decent coach. Along with Coach Mac, he taught us to respect others and to be both good citizens and players. I learned more from Coach Tepper that spring than in all my previous years. He was a real asset to Coach Mac's new staff. We could never figure out how he could see all 11 players at once. He implemented the "same shoulder, same leg" technique for taking on blockers, which instantly made us linebackers harder to block.

Spring practice went well. My 40-yard dash time was now 4.59. To improve my time, I would find the fastest player at my position and run against him. All players need to stretch to increase range of motion and prevent injuries, and Coach Bates always made sure we stretched constantly.

I would have to keep up my grades, and this summer would be the hardest working months of my life. With improved study habits and good, disciplined roommates, I had maintained a 3.5 grade point average or better over my last two years. Taking good notes was key, and starting to review my notes 8 to 10 days before a test helped me to remember the best. By the time the professor had a review a couple days before the test, I had already memorized most everything. I would review 20 to 30 minutes each night the week before, then a little longer up to the day of the test. For years, I had waited until the night before, but never again. I would only cram when absolutely necessary. I had to be prepared.

CHAPTER 64

Terror on the Turnpike

I n all my years at Colorado, one of my best friends was Coach Dan Stavely, almost 80 years old. All of us were thankful to him, as he was thoughtful and always there for us day or night. Anytime we had a problem, Coach Dan would show up.

Coach Dan was active with the Fellowship of Christian Athletes. One day he came into our dining hall asking if any players wanted to go to the Denver Bronco Bible study. In a flash, seven of us were loaded in his car, traveling down the turnpike to Aurora, a Denver suburb. As we arrived, we were greeted by many Bronco players and several All-Pro performers, including Randy Gradishar. Barney Chavous was wonderful to open his house to all of us. We had a great time among these huge, talented athletes. They took us in, treated us like family, and made us feel special. The leader encouraged all of us to be good, clean, godly men around other players and students. After some refreshments and many hugs, we were back on the Boulder Turnpike headed to Boulder.

On the hour-long ride home, I drifted off to sleep. About 30 minutes in, something woke me. I hadn't been the only person asleep – the entire car was out cold, snoring, including our 80-year-old driver. I had to think quick, as we were already over the shoulder. I was in the backseat, so I reached into the front seat and slapped my brother across the back of his head. He was seated just next to the coach, and as I slapped him he startled the coach and woke him up. Ray reached back to beat on me till I motioned to him that the coach had fallen into a deep sleep.

I waited to tell the other players what had happened until after we arrived in Boulder. We all should have been dead. I still thank the Lord as He sent an angel to awaken me. I would have never imagined waking up on the highway only to see every single person sound asleep, driver included. We all laughed about it later.

CHAPTER 65

Summer Training Before My Senior Year

The summer would involve 12 weeks of total dedication, especially with my new incentive as starting inside linebacker. I would still have to work 40-50 hours per week under the hot sun. The Harper brothers, out of Wheat Ridge, were kind enough to hire me year after year to help them roof houses. I was lucky if I could only put on about five pounds during the scorching summer months. Most players are lucky to report back in August weighing the same as when they left in May. Now that I would be in the starting rotation, I would have to sacrifice and be diligent in my training. I would run hills, distance, intervals, and sprints five days a week. I would lift heavy three days a week and do pushups three nights per week (1,000 reps or more total).

During my final team workout just before I left CU for the summer, a player was doing some parallel dips. As he dismounted the bar, he turned to me and yelled, "Cone, when we get back in the fall I'll smash your dip record!" He made the statement in front of the entire team, and I took it as a direct challenge. When I got home that summer, I built a dip bar in my backyard in his honor. I would incorporate an extra night of dips per week and several extra sets that summer just for him! By the end of my summer training, I would do a set of more than 100 thinking only about his challenge.

My 29th Street run through Wheat Ridge was my hardest run each week. I could only do it once per week, and it had to be at night with little traffic. I would put my Impala in gear with the window down, then hop out and run beside it for 1½ miles. My car would cruise at close to 15 mph. The car would stay relatively straight with few corrections. I would sprint the entire distance alongside it. Only two stoplights were en route, and 90 percent of the time they were green. I would pray for no cramping, pulled muscles, potholes, or road kill! It was dangerous but exciting. I often wondered what people thought when they passed me.

My weight training went great. I got in with a group of heavy lifters at Arvada West High School, including Mr. Colorado. They helped me achieve my goals and pushed me to my limits. Even on Saturdays they worked out for four hours, all bringing their own lunches. My bench press was now up to 325 pounds for a set of 20 reps and 405 pounds for a set of 6 reps. My dead lift was now 600 pounds for five reps. I could strap on 180 pounds for 18 reps on parallel dips. My parallel squats were at 505 pounds for five reps, and power cleans were at 315 pounds for five reps. I would leave the gym exhausted only to see my friends stay behind for a couple more hours. As a walk-on, I could never stop, and so I was always exhausted. I finished 500 sit-ups before bed every night by 11 p.m. I would try to stay up long enough to finish my devotions. Oftentimes I would wake up seven hours later in the same exact position I had laid down in.

Late one afternoon in early August, I had just sat down to dinner with my folks when the phone rang. My mom handed me the phone. It was Coach McCartney, very businesslike. He had three questions: "Are you training hard? Is your family well? Are you going to be the best-conditioned athlete?"

I answered each question with an emphatic, "Yes, sir."

He then responded in a stern, clear voice, "Then get up here and sign your scholarship!"

I was in shock! Suddenly my appetite was gone, and I was on the Boulder Turnpike heading to see Coach Mac.

He met me at the door of his office with a hug. Coach Mac told me that he appreciated my hard work, and the money I had earned this summer was now mine to spend. He was a great man, a man concerned for others as much as he was concerned about his football team. Before I left his office, he reached under his desk and threw me a box of New Balance running shoes just delivered from the NB rep. I had written New Balance earlier that summer to let them know that I had plans to win the Best Conditioned Athlete Award that fall for the fourth year in a row. I would train in their shoes and advertise for them if they would send me a pair of their 990s.

The next day, I told my lifting partners at Arvada West about my scholarship. They all celebrated by giving me some of their tuna fish, and then they made me stay for a three-hour workout! I was on cloud nine for the next two weeks, but soon I would have to report for two-a-day practices. I was so proud of my New Balance shoes. I showed them to everyone I knew. The 990 model was so nice that I could train in them and then wear them out to the movies or dinner.

CHAPTER 66

Meeting Adjourned

A fter a late-night summer run around Panorama Park in Wheat Ridge, Colorado, I decided to run two blocks to the east and pay a quick visit to my lifelong friend Jerry Harper. He had taught us how to install roofs during the long, hot summers. As I approached his house, I saw Jerry sitting in his car with a disappointed look on his face.

"What's wrong, bro?" I asked.

In a small voice, he answered, "My wife joined some religion, and I've been kicked out of my own house."

She was having a meeting with her new congregation inside. I owed Jerry big time since he had lent me money all through high school and had let us jump on his trampoline since I was a kid.

"I can fix that," I said. "I'll have that meeting adjourned within minutes."

I took a peek in the backyard, then came back. I told Jerry to sit on the front porch and hold the screen door open. I went around back to the kennel that housed his huge Doberman, Knuckles. Grabbing the overgrown beast by the collar, I lifted him through the back bedroom window.

The rest was history, as all the visitors were out of the house within 30 seconds. Oh, how funny it was, grown men running for their lives. Jerry couldn't thank me enough.

CHAPTER 67

Report Back for Senior Year

I t was scorching hot in the middle of August as we reported back to Boulder for twice-daily practices. The thermometer was near 94 degrees for the entire week with no signs of letting up. After our first team dinner, we would have the evening off. The next morning would be the most physically demanding test of my life. The Best Conditioned Athlete Competition was about to begin. All through the dorm that evening, I heard different strategies on how players would try to win. Many athletes returned looking buffed and sleek. I overheard many claims of running and lifting hard over the summer. Several new recruits as well as junior college transfers were striving to come out on top.

I returned in the best shape of my life, yet I kept quiet. I was getting psyched!

The next morning, it was on. I knew I could eat only a light breakfast, since we would have to run the mile and a half as hard as we could. Everybody had their own body weight coefficient formula and had their own chance to win points in each event. The points would be cumulative over two days. As we began the run, I tactfully didn't start out too fast and kept a solid pace until the end. I finished in fourth place out of 125 players. We then went up to the AstroTurf field and did our 40-yard dash sprint test. The test was to run 16 x 40 yard sprints as hard as we could within one half second of our fastest time from the spring before. Only one minute of rest was allowed after every four sprints. I did well and scored several points.

At the end of the first day, the locker room buzzed since players were dying to know where they stood. Several athletes said, "Just wait – tomorrow we'll separate the men from the boys." That night, I felt that my chances were pretty good and that this summer's hardcore running and lifting regimen was about to pay off. My secret plan was to try to blow every one of them away in every event. We all hung out laughing late that night, and the atmosphere was a little more relaxed now that the running tests were over. Tomorrow would be my chance to excel at the lifting events. I had a surprise for every teammate, and I could hardly wait! I was so jacked up.

The next morning, we were up at dawn. Several players asked me how much I was going to lift and wanted to know how hard I had worked out over the summer. They knew I had won the prestigious award for the last three years. I purposely kept quiet.

I told them I was just thankful to be here and wished them well. We headed down to the weight room, and the weight lifting challenge began.

I asked the Lord for strength and to keep me safe from cramps, muscle pulls, and all injuries. The first test was the body weight bench press. I would blow the entire team away with 38 reps of 225 pounds with a slow four count on each one to eliminate excessive bouncing. During the dip contest, I doubled my closest competition. Remember the dude who was going to smash my dip record? I more than doubled his output with 64, with a four count on each to stop swinging. The chin-up test would be challenging, as we were to take a four count on each chin-up to keep players from swinging. It would be tough, as I knew two wide receivers who could do at least 20 each. Again I blew the field away. I did 30 with a slow four count on each one – the next-closest person was 14 behind me.

At the team meeting that night, Coach Mac made the announcements. He handed out plaques and trophies for each individual event, then a beautiful trophy for the team's Best Conditioned Athlete. "The winner is Marty Cone!" I was so thankful. After all the prayers, hours of training, and thousands of pushups that summer, I had won again. Coach Tepper congratulated me as well, which meant a lot! Now it was back to work as two-a-day practices were at hand, and the season was only a few short weeks away.

CHAPTER 68

Bennett Fracture

———————✦———————

y roommate had a Bryan Adams cassette tape that we would listen to over and over in between two-a-day practices. We would try to sleep whenever we could, usually from about 12:30 to 2:30 in the afternoon before the afternoon practice. It's important to rest as often as you can since you'll be put to the test several hours each day. Tackling, blocking, reads, drops, and conditioning went on for hours each day, then film and more film morning, noon, and night. For two solid weeks we would have a team meeting every night and then head back to the dorm to start over again the next morning.

We would have a scrimmage one week before our opener against Colorado State. As I was tackling our big fullback, my right thumb got caught in his facemask. I felt it burn and swell up right away. I had to go to the hospital in downtown

Denver, only to return with my thumb in a cast. I had a Bennett fracture. A broken right thumb – not a good way to start your senior campaign.

After two-a-days were over, the pain subsided, and I was able to use my cast as a weapon. I would now have to split time at inside linebacker since I was on injured reserve for awhile.

CHAPTER 69

The U-Haul from Heaven

A fter another grueling week of two-a-day practices, my roommate, Tom, and I walked up to the hill area just off the campus to get a tall limeade from Dairy Queen to quench our thirst. Afterward, we had to get back across campus to Tom's car since our afternoon practice would start in about an hour. Wouldn't you know it was parked on the far side of the campus? It was midday, and we both were dragging. We were hoping for a ride since we were on foot.

Enter the U-Haul from heaven. I said to Tom, "I've got a great idea. This U-Haul truck is heading south down Broadway. Let's hop on the back and hang on!"

With four stoplights in front of us, the plan was to jump off at the first red light. It was on! Both of us were on the back bumper holding on to the door strap and to each other. I can't imagine how I talked Tom into getting on there with me! Tom was a pre-med student with a 4.0 grade point average. His dad was the Chancellor of the University of Wisconsin, River Falls.

Suddenly the truck gained speed. I told Tom to relax as our first red light was coming up. To my surprise the truck sailed through a green light at the intersection. With full presence of mind, I told Tom to relax as the next light would be our stop. Then the truck sailed through another green light, then yet another! I told Tom that if the truck turned left on Baseline Avenue we would have to make a jump or we'd wind up in Denver. Sure enough, the truck turned left on Baseline.

And so with the truck going at a high rate of speed, we jumped and then both landed sprinting into the corner gas station. Tom was one step in front of me and leaped over the hood of an elderly woman's car. I wasn't so lucky and smashed right into the driver's side door. I'm sure I scared her half to death when she saw us flying off of a U-Haul truck and heading directly at her. I lay on the ground next to her car door.

She asked me, "What in the hell do you think you're doing?"

I could only answer, "I'm not really sure!"

Tom and I quickly gathered ourselves, got up, and ran for Tom's car. I think I dented her car door. We both could have been seriously hurt, and right in the middle of our two-a-day practices.

People in line at the gas station probably thought we had been shot out of a canon. As we looked back on Baseline Avenue, sure enough the U-Haul truck had made another green light and was now headed up the ramp to Denver. At least we wound up much closer to Tom's car in the east side parking lot.

I often wondered how Coach Mac would have handled the situation if he had found out that I had his starting field goal kicker jumping on the back of a U-Haul and flying across the highway!

CHAPTER 70

Michigan State

Michigan State would be an exciting road trip, as we would land in Detroit City. The first things that came to mind were the Motown sound, sports teams, huge factories, and automobile makers. Soon the bus headed for East Lansing, home of the Michigan State Spartans. Many of us were in awe as we thought about the Big Ten, basketball traditions, and great football. I believe Magic Johnson himself could have run for governor.

The country was thick with trees, rolling hills, and beautiful red barns. The scenery was spectacular. The state patrol gave us a full escort all the way to the stadium as they did on each road trip, and people stood on the side of the road to watch. It always felt amazing to be escorted with sirens blaring and lights flashing. We felt like VIPs.

As we arrived at the campus, literally thousands of people were already filing into the stadium. I kept thinking, wow, what a tradition! This school was huge, and the campus was enchanting on the cool fall day. The entire Spartan basketball team stood next to our bus. I think I counted at least eight guys over 6'6". I knew that players came from all over the Midwest to play here.

Once again, as we took the field, the stadium was absolutely packed. The entire stadium was a sea of white and green with thousands of students and athletes. Most of us felt small and a little intimidated. We were definitely outnumbered. Some of their offensive lineman looked like they were ready for the NFL, huge and strong.

I'll never forget the punt team that day. This would be my most difficult physical test of the early season. I had the hardest time trying to keep one particular blocker off of me. He would be assigned to me all day long. This giant would grab me, hold me, sometimes throw me down, and pancake me. I was furious and frustrated, as he tormented me the entire game. Finally I told him I was going to kick his ass if he didn't get himself off of me. He laughed at me all the way down the field on every punt. Our team worked extremely hard but fell short to a much bigger and more talented team that day.

On Monday's film study, I knew the punt team coach was about to exploit me. Coach Les Miles (Louisiana State

University) pointed out how poorly I had done on the punt team all day long. As he kept making an example out of me, I got more pissed after each comment. He mouthed off to me once again, and I snapped.

I screamed, "You couldn't have blocked his ass either, you jerk."

Right then Coach Miles kicked me off the punt team. I stood up and threw my chair across the room at him, ready to fight. Several players stood up to try to stop me. I stormed out and went looking for Coach Mac, as I knew he would listen to me. I had worked hard to be on the punt team, and no young assistant was going to kick me off without a fight.

I found Coach Mac in a coaches' meeting. He graciously came into the hall to hear me out.

"Me and Miles are gonna fight, and I mean right now!" I said.

Coach Mac told me to relax, and then told me he knew all about the player I had been trying to block, as he had tried to recruit him to Michigan just before he came to Colorado. His name was Carl Banks, who would go on to start for the New York Giants for the next decade on the opposite side of Lawrence Taylor. He would be the third person taken in the NFL draft just a few months later. He stood about 6'5" and weighed about 255 pounds. He was the most gifted athlete for his size that I would ever play against. Players that big and strong should be banned from special teams. I think I counted a fan club of more than 30 people wearing his tee shirt during the game. I had to keep a low profile that next week in practice because Carl Banks had thrown me around like a rag doll.

Coach Mac told me not to worry, and then reinstated me on the punt team. A special thank you to Carl Banks for getting me kicked off the punt team. Also, thank you, Coach Mac.

I remember getting my front tooth knocked out in the third quarter at Michigan State. I had to have the official at midfield stop the game for a few seconds so I could find it. That was Air Force porcelain, and I needed it back. After I found it in the middle of the field, I threw it to Coach Tepper on the sidelines and told him to put it in his pocket.

I would undergo oral surgery after the following Wednesday's practice and have to recover by the next day for practice and a game three days later. What an experience, Michigan State!

CHAPTER 71

The Equipment Bag
That Came to Life

E ach practice for the first month of my senior year, I noticed an equipment bag full of footballs up in front next to the captains. Coach Mac would stand next to this bag and watch all of us stretch near the 50 yard line. I would often wonder if a fully dressed player could fit in this bag. I had to find out.

The next day, two players carried me onto the field inside the bag. They placed the bag in the usual place. I was in that bag for at least five minutes until practice began, popping my head out and making players laugh. You could get in big time trouble for being late to practice, but I reasoned that I was actually five minutes early. I was able to see out through a tiny crack.

Once Coach Mac was standing next to the bag, several players began yelling out, "Where's Cone?" Then they told him to check the bag. He poked the bag with his yardstick as I unzipped the bag and reached out, grabbing his leg. Coach Mac jumped and ran a few steps away.

The players thought it was funny. Coach Mac walked off just shaking his head.

CHAPTER 72

Notre Dame

Notre Dame was possibly the most anticipated event of my entire senior year. The mystique of the fighting Irish alone would fill the stands on Saturday. They had the most storied tradition in the nation. Coach Mac informed us early in the week of just how powerful they were, with almost 70 blue chip All-Americans on their roster. We read every publication and studied more film on them than any other team up to that point.

Friday afternoon, it was on! Notre Dame was in the house. We had just finished our 45-minute walkthrough practice as the Irish took the field for their walkthrough. I don't think any of our players left the field; nobody wanted to miss seeing this historic team. They had the biggest, strongest line we had ever seen. They even brought two priests with them and that goofy-looking mascot. We were simply in awe!

My teammates and I reassured each other that we shouldn't be intimidated and that all we needed to do was knock one of those mammoths to the ground in front of our Boulder fans. It was hard not to be a little nervous because Notre Dame had access to the top players in the country, many of whom were here.

The next day, the locker room was a little too quiet. I started to scream and told the team what I was going to do to those big, fat giants! It seemed to take the edge off, and other players joined in. There was a nice arm curl machine in the weight room right by the door to the field. To get pumped up, I would always do at least 10 sets before going onto the field. I didn't start at linebacker since I was still in a lot of pain with my broken thumb, hip pointer, bruised AC joint, and gum surgery, but I would be in the game early.

In the middle of the first quarter, Coach Tepper yelled, "Cone, you're in!" I sprinted in as fast as could, running on a cloud of air. As they broke the huddle and lined up in front of me, I had to catch my breath and calm my nerves. I had never seen a more powerful group of linemen. Before they hiked the ball, I got a firsthand look at what the top tight end in the country looked like. His name was Mark Bavaro, who would later be the starting tight end for the New York Giants. The quarterback would play in the pros for the next 15 years. The running back would get second place in the Heisman voting and play in the NFL. For now, I would have to concentrate on my immediate responsibility, filling A and B gaps if it were a run and covering two drop zones if it were a pass.

The first play was a run to the right, only gaining a few yards. The second play was a pass to the flats, which we managed to stop. On the third play, I was called on a blitz up the middle. I had studied the film and felt that this blitz would work, as the guard and tackle had extremely wide splits. I stacked behind the tackle instead of the guard, figuring if this behemoth of a guard didn't see me over him, I could loop around him and get into the backfield before he noticed me. As the ball was snapped, I made a beeline to hit the guard-center (A) gap. From the backfield I busted the running back for a four-yard loss.

As I stood over my victim, I screamed, "Welcome to the Big Eight," which was our standard greeting. While screaming, I accidentally threw up part of a pancake on him. Bits of it landed on his facemask and on his face. He was furious and complained to the referee. I told the ref that the Harvest House restaurant had overfed us and that I couldn't hold it in because I was nervous about the fighting Irish being in the house. At halftime, I apologized to the refs again, and now I had the whole group laughing.

We fought as hard as we could against a much more physical team. They had a lot of big players out of Pennsylvania and Ohio that year. Their coach was a good friend of our Coach Mac, both having ties to the popular Moeller High School in Cincinnati, Ohio. We never forgot the day the mighty Irish came to town. We played well, yet fell short by a couple of touchdowns. I thought about that game for many years.

CHAPTER 73

Iowa State Cyclones

———————❖———————

A pretty smooth flight got us safely into Des Moines to take on the Cyclones. The weather was cold, rainy, and miserable. As we arrived at the stadium on Friday afternoon, we got all taped up for our easy walkthrough practice. As our team entered the field, Iowa State's team was just leaving. The last player off the field was the Cyclones quarterback. He had on some real nice Iowa State warm-ups. Big George, our defensive tackle, was by my side as I confronted the opposing quarterback. I told him I was here for one reason: to jump off sides and bash him in the neck when he tried a quarterback sneak.

"Isn't that right George?" I asked.

George just nodded. George was intimidating. He was from Waimanalo, Hawaii, and was around 6'4" and 260 pounds. He worked as a spear fisherman during the summer.

Iowa State's quarterback said, "What do you want from me?"

I answered, "Give me your Iowa State football shirt and shorts, and I'll call off the dogs!" To my surprise, he took off his shirt and gave it to me. We had only been bluffing.

George and I went to the field and started stretching with the team. Five minutes later Iowa State's team manager came running up to Coach Mac and asked him where #45 was. Coach pointed to where I was stretching. Their manager came over and threw me the quarterback's shorts. I couldn't believe it. We all were dying laughing. Now I had a complete set of Iowa State football warm-ups.

The next morning the game was on. It was raining, and water covered the sidelines. The temperature couldn't have been more than 40 degrees. Coach Tepper made all of us linebackers dive and roll through puddles of freezing water to get ready to play. I couldn't believe he would do that to us, but it worked. It made us ready to play this much-improved team.

Iowa State had a pretty balanced attack with two good running backs and a quarterback who was up for All Big Eight honors. Late in the third quarter, Iowa State had the ball on our 30 yard line. It was fourth down and one yard to go. They went for it. I had studied the film all week, and I knew what the play was going to be. The quarterback would always run a quarterback sneak over his big, strong, left guard anytime there was short yardage. Sure enough, there he came. I met him in midair and stopped him in his tracks. After our midair collision, I never saw much of the Iowa State quarterback. We kept the ball for most of the fourth quarter.

As the game ended, I walked off the field with Big George. I got a tap on the shoulder. I looked back and saw the Iowa State quarterback wearing a neck brace.

He said, "I thought you said you wouldn't bash my neck if I gave you my warm-ups."

Big George and I both were speechless. I guess I had hurt their quarterback on the fourth and one quarterback sneak. We both apologized and shook his hand. We let him know that it all had been a joke. The next year, 6'3" Dave Archer would be the starting quarterback for the Atlanta Falcons. I still kept his warm-ups!

CHAPTER 74

The Face of an Angel

<hr>

F all semester my senior year I took a great history class on Indians and the Old West with my roommate, Tom. Our professor was said to be one of the country's foremost experts on Indian history. It was the fourth week of the season.

My right hand was still in a plaster cast due to my broken thumb; however, the cast had been modified to where I could take it off and on to take notes. I would sit at the back of the class where I could take my cast off. I guess the odor wasn't too pleasant, at least according to some girls sitting nearby.

I was leaning on my left arm, taking notes and minding my own business as usual. Next to me sat the "angel," Tom, the perfect All American student. Everybody thought he was so innocent, but I knew better. Tom, the sly fox that he was, slapped my left arm away from my head. I went flying out of my desk onto the ground, books and all. It must have sounded like a car wreck. The class was laughing, and I was so embarrassed lying there on the ground.

The professor yelled, "Out, get out of my class!" I felt sorry for Tom, the straight A pre-med student, because he was going to have to leave. Then, with a little more dispatch, the professor said, "You, in the Powerlifting USA tee-shirt, out!" Now I was mad because I was the one who had to leave the class. I grabbed my books, jacket, cast, and ACE bandages. As I got to the door, I glared at Tom to subliminally say "thank you!" There he sat with the face of an angel as if he had done nothing wrong!

I met with the professor afterwards, and he said the incident was no big deal. I however, still wanted to scalp Tom.

CHAPTER 75

Nebraska Cornhuskers

Back during two-a-days, we put Nebraska in red letters on our game schedule. Now came our red-letter week, as we would face the Nebraska Cornhuskers. The entire season led up to this game. Nebraska may have been the best team in the country that year. Our plane trip was unusually quiet. Most players were extremely focused, especially now that Nebraska was sporting two Outland trophy winners and that year's Heisman Trophy winner. They were loaded with talent, mostly in state recruits. Almost every high school athlete would love to play for the Huskers, though every now and then we would be able to sweet talk a Nebraska recruit to join the Buffs.

As the state patrol escorted our bus to the field, we were high with anticipation. When we began our walkthrough the day before the game, a sea of red was already forming. The stadium was in downtown Lincoln, which is kind of weird since fans walk downtown right into an ugly gray stadium. I was awestruck as I saw the Huskers' weight room and workout facilities. Trophies, national championships, and records hung all over the walls. Their weight room was as big as a grocery store. It seemed to me that every successful businessman, farmer, or worker in Nebraska stood behind the Huskers.

Before our team took the field for Saturday's game, I went out early with the specialists (kickers and punters) just to get a look at what was going on. Everyone wore red, from grandparents down to newborn babies. I felt if the fans got mad at us they might overrun the field, and we would be history.

As I retrieved balls for the field goal kicker, I looked around at this venue. It was a spectacle to behold. It seemed like the entire state of Nebraska was there. After about 30 minutes, I met the rest of our team as we took the field. During warm-ups, I saw a big group of players in the Nebraska end zone. I could hardly believe my eyes – their team was already on the field. These men were the linemen only, a group of 30-40 guys all looking like they weighed 270 pounds or better. Their freshman could have all started on our offensive line. It was hard for a lot of us to concentrate, as we couldn't figure out where Nebraska had gotten so many huge players. They had more depth than any other school I had seen in the past four years. It was a strange feeling, almost eerie. I knew good and well that all our players were caught up in the flow of the Huskers being in the national championship hunt.

In the first quarter, Nebraska broke the huddle and lined up over the ball. I was actually more nervous than when we played Notre Dame. I would have to face the center and left guard, each of whom had won the Outland Trophy for the nation's top lineman. The tailback would go on to win the Heisman; the fullback, wide receiver, and other lineman would all be in the NFL for years to come. They fired out hard and low to the ground, and when I got up others would knock me down again. It was very physical, as Boyd Epley's strength program was the best in the nation. I felt like a stick figure against these muscled animals! I recalled that before we headed to Nebraska, a friend who played for the University of New Mexico called long distance from Albuquerque to give us some bad news. He said that when they recently played against Nebraska, the Huskers' offensive line had told the New Mexico players where they were going to run the ball. The problem was that there was nothing the New Mexico players could do about it.

Coach Mac and his staff had worked endlessly that week to put in a single back set, which gave us an extra blocker. Just before halftime, we were actually ahead, 12-10. The third quarter is when the wheels fell off. We fumbled a kickoff at the goal line. Next possession, we got intercepted at the 10, and then we fumbled. And so on. By the start of the fourth quarter, we were down by 35 points. During the fourth quarter, they had their third team offensive guard in. This would be one of the fiercest players I had ever played against. Powerful and vicious, he would block, grab, push, and fight. The entire fourth quarter he was relentless, and it was hard to keep him off me. I found out later he had lost his starting job and was real mad about it. This just shows how deep Nebraska was at each position.

My hat went off to Tom Osborne and the Husker program. They were going to be on top for many years to come. I admired Coach Mac all the more, as we played many superior teams back to back. He always made us believe that were we just as good as they were.

I also recall that the crowd wasn't very nice. They seemed to have an attitude. I saw a lot of things on this trip that I would remember the rest of my life.

CHAPTER 76

Marty and Tom's Pancake House

I was now living off campus, and my roommate was still good ol' Tom. We finally backed off each other since we got tired of knocking each other out. He was still my best friend. One day as we walked through an alley a block from our apartment, we heard voices coming from an abandoned garage nearby. Out popped Ralph, a tall, slender, bearded dude with scraggly blonde hair. He was about 40 years old. We befriended him and found out he was living in the unheated garage with two others friends. We invited them over for pancakes the next morning.

They arrived at 8 a.m. sharp. We ushered them in from the cold. I had about six pancakes going at once. As fast as I would set them out, they would eat them. We found out that Ralph hadn't had a warm breakfast in days. Bless his heart, the poor guy was just trying to survive. We encouraged him and his two friends to hang in there, as we all walked out and Tom and I left for class. I had had to eat eggs that day because Ralph alone had wolfed down 80 percent of our pancakes! No problem, as that night we bought more mix so we could enjoy a full batch the next morning by ourselves.

At 8 a.m. the next day, we heard a light tap on the door. We weren't happy about it because it was our only day to sleep in. Tom and I both got up and answered the door. Sure enough, it was Ralph along with four more friends. I guess word had spread. We couldn't turn these poor guys away, so we asked them in, and I whipped up a batch of pancakes as Tom set the table for the whole crew! There was no batter left after Ralph's happy clan were all fed. We told them we were sorry, but we couldn't host breakfast every day. We all prayed together, and we sent them on their way. As they left, one of them told me my missing tooth made me look like a monster. What a thing to say to the hands that fed him!

The next week on Thursday night we had a Bible study in our living room. Attendance was high, as many of our friends stopped in. We were about 15 minutes into the lesson when we heard a little tap on the door. It was Ralph. He had taken us up on a previous offer to study God's Word. I felt good at first, hoping that Ralph could lean on one of God's promises and perhaps have another chance at a more productive life. As we all sat there quietly, however, Ralph began to act up.

He tried to grasp the air as if he were fighting some demon. Next, he got up and stomped on the floor. When he touched a girl's hair, it was over. I gave him every opportunity to calm down, but he wouldn't. We realized that our poor friend was suffering from mental illness. We put two sandwiches in a paper bag and said goodbye to our friend, and the study resumed.

Ralph would stop by a few more times that semester since we promised to help him whenever he was hungry, and we always gave him food and saved our old clothing for him and his friends.

CHAPTER 77

Missouri Tigers

———————◦•◦———————

M issouri would be the greatest physical test I would ever endure. Their offensive line was the toughest I had ever faced. All five interior linemen were focused. Two or three of them would receive All Big Eight honors. If they had a chance to hit me, they would try to drive me into the ground. Their offensive guards would hunch way down low in their stance, which made them that much harder to escape. Other teams were as big, but no team had as much savage intensity as did Missouri that year.

Early in the game my personal injuries began to mount. I got an AC joint bruise in the middle of the first quarter. That's when the upper shoulder swells up a couple of inches and feels like it's broken. By the start of the second quarter, we all felt ravaged as the Tigers overran us. At halftime, the coaches were screaming at us and putting in changes. In the third quarter, I got my second hip pointer of the season, and my head was bashed so hard that I lay on the Astroturf for a moment and had to come out of the game for a play. I had to convince the coaches I was fit enough to return.

I had a game-high 22 tackles, but I had to work for every single one of them. My hat goes off to Missouri. They didn't appear to be that dominating on the films, but they beat us soundly! Their offensive line was as good as Nebraska, maybe better.

That game, we were weak at nose guard. He had cried during our two-a-day practices, confessing that he had broken up with his girlfriend and could hardly eat or work out. He had lost 30 pounds over the summer, but for some reason he was still the starter at only 225 pounds. Most of us were furious at him, as we had all paid a difficult price to maintain our weight and strength over the summer. Usually you have to double-team a nose guard, but I believe Missouri realized it wasn't necessary. Because of him, one extra lineman had been allowed to wreak havoc on us linebackers all day.

After the game, a guy from a local Boulder radio station asked if I would meet him in the locker room for a live radio interview. In the locker room, they put a live headset on me while they were talking to a caller who had a few things to say.

He rambled, saying, "It's obvious CU doesn't have any linebackers," along with other nonsense.

While the caller was still on the line, I was asked to speak. I was furious and could hardly control my words. I said, "It's not a linebacker problem, it's a nose guard problem. The linebackers fought for our lives the entire game!" I reminded the caller that it's the nose guard's job to try to keep us linebackers free. Then the caller insisted that I was weak. Oh boy, it was on! I told him to come down to the practice fields on Tuesday, and I would give him a chance to take my position. Then he mumbled something else stupid about our team and my head coach. I wasn't about to let that stand, so I responded, "Listen you pencil neck, I'd like to pull you right through this microphone and beat your ass."

That was it. I was asked to leave, no further questions. I told the station to take a stand or find some other softy to interview. I was never asked on that radio program again, which was fine by me! At least our main station, radio 850, always showed respect, and I would have several opportunities to comment live on their show. Former CU great and Denver Bronco Bobby Anderson would always stop by for a live interview.

The next morning, my body was so bruised that two teammates had to help me out of bed. They got me to my car, where I was able to drive to the training room and crawl into the hot tub for a solid hour. The next Wednesday, I got knocked down and landed on my buttocks during practice. I was unable to get up, and the trainers found out that I had a bad bruise leftover from the Missouri game. I didn't know that I had hurt myself that badly. Now my next week's starting spot at inside linebacker would be in jeopardy.

CHAPTER 78

The Eyewitness

———◦———

I t was late October, and my body was still sore all over from the Missouri game. On a cool 40 degree night, I thought I would go for a nice peaceful jog to try to alleviate some pain. It was the first time I had a chance to wear my new stereo headphones. I was halfway around campus, near the "hill" area, when I thought I heard a crash. I stopped. Sure enough, I looked across Broadway, and in a parking lot, underneath the Art Hardware building, I saw a red Mustang parked on top of a yellow Volkswagen. As I started across Broadway, the Mustang backed up and sped away. I was able to get a make and description of the car and the plates.

Now I was off to find the owner of the Volkswagen. I went inside the Art Hardware building and was told that the car's owner was a gal named Linda, who was in a drawing class

238

upstairs. I went upstairs and knocked on the classroom door, then walked into a class of 30 students all focused on a subject at the front of the class. That subject was a naked woman named Linda.

As I told her what had happened to her car, she got slightly hysterical. She rushed to the window to see for herself. I reassured her that I could help as I had witnessed the accident, then I encouraged her to get dressed and said I would accompany her downstairs. The Boulder police were notified and took a report. We then returned to the classroom, where a nude dude had taken her spot.

I left and returned to my peaceful run. Back at our apartment, my roommates assured me that only I would "literally" run into a situation like that.

CHAPTER 79

Non-Certified Athletic Trainer

A fter watching our ankles getting taped for several years, I had another beautiful idea. I had at least 20 rolls of tape in my football locker, along with pre-wrap and lubricant. I also had several willing accomplices who were tired of coming in hours early to get their ankles taped. It was on. I took responsibility for taping up seven of us before practice. I set up a table to display my handiwork back in the laundry room of the team house. The first three tapings of the week went off without a hitch.

However, missing taping was a big no-no, as your name needed to be crossed off a list before practice started. Before Thursday's practice out on the field, Coach Mac called seven of us up in front of the team. Then the head trainer called us all out one by one. All seven of us were now on trial. We were told to remove our cleats and our socks. Coach Mac and the eight different trainers were all puzzled, as our ankles were taped to perfection. The entire team was laughing during the inquisition. All the different trainers took a close look to see if they recognized their taping jobs. My pupil, Derrick, from Novato, California, was just as guilty for taping me. No one could figure out who had done the taping.

Just then, the team manager came running out onto the field with a bag of leftover supplies of tape he had found buried in the bottom of my locker. He wanted to show the entire staff. Suddenly our cover was blown.

Coach Mac asked me in front of the team what I thought I was doing. I replied, "Only trying to help, coach. Can I tape all you coaches tomorrow?" Coach Mac walked away shaking his head, and the inquisition was over. The case of the mysterious athletic trainer was solved. What was the harm in trying to help out with my new skill, anyway?

CHAPTER 80

Second Trip to Norman, Oklahoma

W e all knew that Oklahoma would have their usual outstanding team. The night before the game, I was lying in our hotel room bed at 11 p.m., wide awake. Curfew was now in effect, but I wanted to take in every minute of fun. I couldn't get to sleep for the life of me, and I was really hungry, so I got dressed and went down the hall to look for any volunteers to sneak away for a hamburger. Two young freshmen players joined me on a late-night escapade. I didn't have much to lose, as I wasn't starting linebacker that week due to slow recovery from the Missouri beating the week before.

Three of us walked down the street after curfew. I told the young freshmen to keep quiet and not to do anything to get us in trouble. It was pretty bad to go out after curfew, but if we were caught I figured I would blame it on the freshmen. The staff might understand that I had to feed and protect the younger classmen. Naturally the two freshmen had no money, so I would have to treat. As we crossed the highway to the burger stand, I noticed a familiar sight. To our surprise, another one of our players, Dan McMillan, was already there, enjoying a king-sized hamburger.

We all laughed and ate until we were full. A van came up loaded with four women and two dudes. They asked if we wanted a ride. They gave us a short tour of the main drag to show us all the excitement about the next day's game against Colorado. They asked us what we were doing in Norman. I said that we would be working on the field for the game. Not long after, they dropped us off near the hotel. They were polite and sweet.

The girl driving the van asked, "Why am I dropping you off behind your hotel?"

"We're actually playing for the Colorado Buffs tomorrow," I said, "and we're out after curfew, so now we have to sneak back inside." The entire van thought that was pretty cool. We loved everyone in that van. We told them our jersey numbers and said we would see them tomorrow. After we snuck back inside the hotel, we had a pushup contest until about 1 a.m., just having a good time messing around.

243

The next day before the game, we were on the field. Our new friends from the night before came down in a huge pack to say hello near the sidelines. I climbed over the rail and hugged at least 15 girls.

Barry Switzer had his usual top five team with many players heading to the pros the following season. I was standing on the sidelines with my two fellow perpetrators as the game began. The temperature was about 65 degrees, and the day was absolutely beautiful. We spotted our dear friend Tony Casillas and waved to him. I could see him smiling through his facemask.

On the third play of the game, our starting inside linebacker took on one of the Sooner running backs and was knocked to the ground. He had to be helped off the field because he had a severely bruised sternum. The fourth play of the game, I was back in my starting position. As my name was called, I sprinted onto the field as fast as I could. Before the first snap of the ball, I looked back at my two freshman accomplices, only to see a look of terror on both of their faces. They weren't sure I would be able to perform after goofing off into the late-night hours.

Coach Tepper had a brilliant defensive plan, as he would have me blitz three out of every four downs. We would match Oklahoma touchdown for touchdown. On the play just before half, the Sooners tailback punched me in the throat. It hurt bad. I tapped the ref on the shoulder, he looked back. I was unable to speak, so I pointed to my throat in the hopes that he had seen the cheap shot. I guess I couldn't get my point across, so the ref must have thought I was some kind of nut. During halftime, I could hardly swallow, but I finally regained my voice, and I told the ref what the player had done. The ref assured me he would keep an eye on him.

We fought and fought the second half and had them close in the fourth quarter. I was happy to make their head coach Barry Switzer a little nervous. I may have had the best game of the year, ending up with 15 tackles. Still, they wore us down through the fourth quarter and beat us by a couple of touchdowns. We spent most the game trying to figure out how Switzer could recruit so many star athletes. My hat goes off to him, along with his entire staff and all their Heisman hopefuls.

I left the showers early to get to the parking lot. Many Sooner fans were still parked and eating leftovers, so I invited myself over. Oklahoma fans were respectful and friendly. I had a great time with them, and they were much more genuine than the Nebraska fans. One girl promised to come out to Colorado and go skiing with us. I waited for five years; I guess she lost my number. It was also good to see my Aunt Nan from Moore, Oklahoma, along with many of her Baptist friends.

CHAPTER 81

Lights, Action, No Camera

———⁂———

C oach Mac was all business as we assembled for our Monday afternoon meeting. He was mad at how our team had played, and he let everybody know about it. Many players were afraid they could be in danger of losing their starting position. Coach Mac implied that many players were dogging it, and the film would show exactly who the culprits were.

I was seated in the middle of the aisle with my arm resting on the film projector – the projector that held all the evidence against my fellow teammates. I nudged my little freshman buddies sitting to my left and told them to watch me. I carefully unscrewed the lens with my right hand. My fellow teammates couldn't believe what I just had just done. At the end of the row sat a tall, lean, outstanding wide receiver named Jon Embree. His dad had played for the Denver Broncos. When I showed him the lens, he just about fainted. Years later, Jon Embree would become the head coach of this very team. Mac chewed on us for 15 minutes more, assuring us that nobody had a position locked up.

Coach Mac then told Coach Tepper to start the film. As the lights dimmed and the action started, the film was a blur. "What's the problem?" Coach Mac asked. Coach Tepper answered, "There's no lens."

Assistant Coach Jim Caldwell (Indianapolis Colts, Detroit Lions) quickly got on his knees, crawling around beside me to help look for the lens. Coach Mac was absolutely beside himself and said that the projector had worked just fine a half hour ago. After a minute or two, I stood up and said, "Hey Coach Mac, look what I found." I held up the lens. After a short pause, the entire room broke into laughter. According to eyewitness accounts, even Coach Mac had his head down, laughing.

You can learn something from each game film, so it's important to pay attention. No goofing off.

Chapter 82

Survivor at the Laundromat

I t was late in the fall, and I was getting low on clothing, as there were now three full bags of dirty laundry in my closet. I had jackets and a large bedspread that needed washing as well. My mom agreed to meet me at the local Laundromat in Wheat Ridge.

It was good to see my mom, a mother of seven, to catch up and talk about old times. The Laundromat was packed with many families and small kids. Now was my chance to show my mom that I was a true "survivor," able to do my own wash and handle anything life could throw my way. As I loaded up this huge rug-washer, I noticed that the hatch door opened from the front, sort of like a submarine. I had never seen a front-loading machine like this before. It was colossal. I put in two little boxes of powdered soap, closed the door, and started her up.

Nearly five minutes went by as I sat there chatting with my mom. Then I realized I had forgotten to load the final bag down at my feet. I wondered how fast I could open the door and throw these garments into the wash. Well here goes, I thought.

I opened the door at record speed and threw the clothing in while my mom screamed. I figured that I could somehow hold the water back with the clothes that I was stuffing in. I couldn't believe how fast all that water gushed out onto the floor. The other people in the Laundromat all had to jump on dryers to avoid the oncoming flood. They were furious. I apologized, but there was nothing I could do. I couldn't tell if my mom was laughing or crying.

When everything had dried, I kissed my mom goodbye, wondering if she really thought I was a survivor. As I stood there in my soaking wet tennis shoes, I knew she was on her way home to tell my dad.

CHAPTER 83

University of Kansas

———————✦———————

Ialways looked forward to playing in Lawrence, Kansas. Their campus is one of the most beautiful in the country. I felt it was second only to Boulder. (Nebraska was dead last.) The Jayhawk's field sits down in a beautiful valley with a picturesque backdrop. A large, grassy area leads up to the memorial at the top of the hill. Hundreds of people were always on the grassy area, and they would all migrate towards the gates just before the game. The student body all wore the beautiful blue Kansas color. Just before we were to take the field, I imagined Wilt Chamberlain and Gayle Sayers playing at this historic venue. I thought of the famous miler Jim Ryan, who had motivated me as a kid. The fans were yelling out, "Rock Chalk, Jayhawk!"

I looked at the roster before the game and realized Kansas had many players from California. All game long, our players yelled at opposing players who had played either with them or against them in high school or junior college in California. It was a pretty cool experience to see good friends playing across the ball from each other. I heard, "That's my homeboy!" all game long. Some were high school teammates, some were cousins, some were crosstown rivals.

It was a hard-fought game. The Jayhawks had quick running backs who were hard to tackle. It was a great road trip. After the game, I grabbed a fellow player and headed to the parking lot where many Kansas fans were still tailgating. They fed us hot dogs, sandwiches, and anything else they had. These were our favorite kinds of fans, always respectful and down to earth, just like the fans in Oklahoma. If I didn't live in Colorado, I would have tried to make it at the University of Kansas. My uncle Harlas would always drive 70 miles from Liberty, Missouri, to watch us play.

Thanks to all the Jayhawks' fans. You were so much nicer than Nebraska.

CHAPTER 84

Kansas State

O ur home game against the Kansas State Wildcats would be the last of my career. Many things went through my mind all week long, as it would be the last week of practice also. On Thursday of that week, we had senior hit day after practice, where seniors would call out the names of the players they wanted to hit. Seniors hyped it up all week long to try to scare the players they were going to hit. My choice was John "Pup" Nairn, a talented freshman who had followed Coach Mac from Michigan.

Players couldn't wait to see the big hit I was about to inflict on the little "Pup." Little did they know that I loved John, as he was a great friend. I had rehearsed with him before practice how I wanted it to go. After all the seniors had exacted punishment on their younger victims, I was the last to go. I yelled out

"Bring on Pup Nairn." Instead of moving back 5 yards, I moved back 10. As Coach Mac blew the whistle, "Pup" ran at me as hard as he could. I stood still, letting him clobber me. From six feet away, Pup knocked me to the ground. The entire team laughed. Coach Mac walked off just shaking his head again.

I always wondered if Nebraska had their own senior corn-husking day.

During my last game, Kansas State was big and fast. The third play of the game I hit the running back with my facemask, causing a fumble. Now they would have to punt. I got up off the ground with blood streaming from my nose, later to find out that my nose was broken. The game went back and forth. During the third quarter, I stopped the Wildcats running back at our five yard line and caused my second fumble of the game. During the fourth quarter, Coach Tepper let me call the plays for defense.

Then it all came to an end. Many of us seniors walked off the field slowly, thanking as many fans as we could, as we realized this would be our last time playing on this sacred field. My emotions were mixed, but I was glad the season was over. My body needed rest and healing. My broken thumb would be sore for the next six months. A custom crown for my broken tooth was now being made. My hip was sore from two hip pointers in the last four weeks. The AC joint in my shoulder was still swollen. It would take several months for the Astroturf scars on my arms to heal. My broken little fingers would now start to mend. I'm sure every player in the Big Eight Conference and all who have played college football would have a similar list.

I was thankful to have been a part of such a class-act team. My younger brother Ray would go on to set the single-season tackle record for the golden Buffs and sign with the Denver Broncos. Thank you to the University of Colorado!

CHAPTER 85

The Cone Brothers on Draft Day

C ome draft day there's always excitement in the house. We expected two of my fellow teammates to be drafted on this very day. David Tate and Mickey Pruitt were two hard-nose defenders, and they were finally about to be recognized for all their hard work. There was only one problem, and my brother Ray and I were about to exploit it.

You see, both players answered the phone every time it rang, so we decided to call them early and often on draft day. I started by phoning Mickey.

I said, "Son, do you like Detroit City?"

He proudly exclaimed, "Yes sir, I do."

I then asked Mickey if he loved the smooth Motown sound. He heard everyone laughing in the background, and he figured out it was the Cone Brothers at it again.

"Leave me alone, Cones, it's draft day," was all he could say.

Now it was David's turn. Ray called and asked for David. In a deep coaches' voice, Ray asked him, "David, do you like the San Diego Chargers?"

David could barely speak. All he could say is "Yes, sir, I do."

Ray responded, "Well then come with us Cone Brothers to San Diego for spring break." David laughed, but he asked us to please stop pranking him on draft day.

We actually did stop. After only three or four more rounds with each one, that is. I called Mickey back and sang, "Please come to Boston for the spring time," only to hear, "Leave me alone, Cone." We called David back and asked him if he liked San Francisco and the Golden Gate Bridge, only to hear, "Leave me alone, Cone." We called Mickey back and asked if he liked Mardi Gras down New Orleans way, only to hear, "Leave me alone, Cone."

They were both signed by the Chicago Bears and had great careers in the NFL. They are both great dudes. We were so proud of them.

CHAPTER 86

The Last Laugh

A few weeks after the season was over, more pro scouts came to town. Perhaps they were looking for a sleeper or someone they may have overlooked for the upcoming NFL draft. I was notified that I was due in front of several scouts at 3:10 pm that very day. I had nothing to lose, as reality had already set in – I knew I had to finish school and then find a job. I arrived at the locker room at 3 p.m. sharp. There were two more players in front of me. No shoes or shirts were allowed, only sweat pants. I had one last chance to try to impress these scouts. Each meeting lasted only about five minutes, and I had to come up with something to get their attention and help my cause.

My brother Ray was just under 6'3" while I was 6'0", so I borrowed his basketball warm-up pants. I unzipped them at the ankles so they would spread and cover my feet. My plan was to stand on my tiptoes for the five-minute interview.

As I arrived in the interview room, I walked in on my toes with as much grace and elegance as I could muster. I was now face to face with 16 pro scouts, each representing a different NFL team. The scouts were all seated as they asked me to stand up in front of the height chart. At first they weren't sure if I was Ray or Marty, as I stood at 6'2". They held up their stat sheets and inundated me with several extra questions, taking a new interest in me. Nobody in the room had known I was that tall; I hadn't even known it since I had only been 6'2" for three minutes.

By now, the meeting had lasted eight minutes. They asked me a battery of questions about my career. How long could I stay up there against that wall on my tiptoes, I wondered? Finally after close to ten minutes my right calf cramped up, which caused my right side to dip. My cover was blown. The famous Dallas Cowboy scout, Gil Brandt, was out of his seat and in my face. He grabbed his yardstick, reached down, and lifted up my warm-up pants, only to find me up on my toes. He called me a name and told me to get the hell out of there. I had to limp out because my calves had cramped. I could hardly make it to the training room where Ted Layne once again came to my rescue and helped to rub me out.

The entire training facility was laughing as I told them what I had attempted. I promptly returned the warm-ups to my brother, as I was now officially done with football. A few hours later at the dining hall, I saw many of the coaches laughing. They wanted to hear my account again. Coach Mac walked away, just shaking his head.

Chapter 87

Farewell

M y final spring semester was by far the most enjoyable because now I could relax and become a regular student. The rigors of the Big Eight conference athletic competition were now over. I was free to exercise, study, and see Boulder in a different light. I would go on to graduate that spring with almost all A's my senior year – a pretty good ending to my long-awaited dream come true. I sincerely hope that I didn't show any disrespect to fellow students, teachers, coaches, or citizens along the way. The late-night howling and pushup contests in the library were meant to just keep us awake.

I want to thank the people who told me I was finished eight years earlier. I have no hard feelings.

Here's what I've learned. You'll have to pay a price to succeed. I remember working 15 hours a week and still playing three sports in high school. I had to work if I wanted a car or if I needed extra money. Now I see high school kids sleeping in until noon (it's due to a growth spurt, their parents say). Hardly anybody works over the month-long Christmas break anymore. Now video games dominate kids' spare time. As God sends snow during the winter, I hardly ever see kids out shoveling to earn a little extra dough. I see parents letting kids off and spoiling them. I just don't see young athletes paying the price and striving to become all they can be. Most are content to just get by.

There's no substitute for hard work. My respect goes out to the true hard workers who have been committed to doing it on their own. My respect goes out to the ones who made it, to the ones who didn't, and to the ones who at all times gave their best. To all my fellow walk-ons in America in any sport, more power to you. You all have a story to tell.

Remember, life is about respect. It's about having respect for your parents, honoring them, and loving them no matter what. It's about respecting what they have to say, even if it sounds old-fashioned. It's about showing respect for your girlfriend or boyfriend. It's about being moral in your behavior. It's about showing respect to your professors, coaches, and friends. It's about encouraging others by telling them you appreciate all their hard work. It's also about respecting your country through thick and thin.

The most important lesson I learned through all my endeavors is to give all the Glory to God. It's not about me, as I have learned that God has set out a roadmap for us to follow, a course for our daily lives. That roadmap is found in the Bible, in His written Word. This way forward is through Jesus Christ, who died on the cross for our sins. He paid the price for us so that we can have Eternal Life. This is my most cherished encouragement for anyone. If you put your faith in Jesus Christ, He will make straight your path. He will open doors and give you the desires of your heart. Following God's Word will help you find true happiness and real success. As is written in Joshua 1:8, "Keep this Book of the Law always on your lips; meditate on it day and night, so that you may be careful to do everything written in it. Then you will be prosperous and successful."

Each campus has lots to offer as far as good, clean, wholesome fun. You'll find campus ministries of the Fellowship of Christian Athletes, Young Life, Campus Crusade for Christ, and Navigators. Get involved in them. You'll have experiences that you'll remember for the rest of your life.

Lord Bless You,
Marty Cone

This book is also dedicated to my dear brother Ray, who was with me every step of the way since we were little boys. We had a great run, and I couldn't have done it without him. We lost Ray before I had a chance to finish this book. He is now resting in peace until we see him again.

May God bless you, Ray. I thank you, I love you, and I miss you more than you could ever know. Blessings to his family.